CAMBRIDGESHIRE
Village Book

*Compiled by the Cambridgeshire Federations of
Women's Institutes from notes and illustrations sent
by W.I.s in the County*

Published jointly by
Countryside Books, Newbury
and the Cambridgeshire Federations
of Women's Institutes: Cambridge,
Isle of Ely, and Huntingdon & Peterborough

First published 1989
New expanded edition 1999
© Cambridgeshire Federations of Women's Institutes 1999

COUNTRYSIDE BOOKS
3 Catherine Road
Newbury, Berkshire

ISBN 1 85306 557 3

Designed by Graham Whiteman

Front and back cover photos of Hemingford Abbots
supplied from the East of England Tourist Board Collection

Produced through MRM Associates Ltd., Reading

Printed by J. W. Arrowsmith Ltd., Bristol

🍁 FOREWORD

Cambridgeshire is a county of waterways. Its rivers flow through chalk hills in the south and wooded claylands in the west to become the almost unique network of embanked rivers and large drainage channels of the now drained Fenland of the north-east of the county. Two cathedrals can be seen, one on the western edge of the Fenland at Peterborough and the other at Ely on the Isle of Ely often called 'The Ship of the Fens'.

The University City of Cambridge is well known, but the rural areas and their villages have many claims to historic interest and beauty.

The Prehistoric trade route, Icknield Way, runs along the chalk ridge in the south east, linking East Anglia and Central England. The Roman road, Via Devana, from Colchester through Cambridge links, at Godmanchester, with Ermine Street from Royston and becomes the Great North Road.

The WI Members and friends who have contributed to this book have enjoyed researching their village histories. There will be a warm welcome to all visitors from those who live in, and care for, these interesting and lovely villages.

Eileen Webster
Co-ordinator

❧ ACKNOWLEDGEMENTS

The three Federations of Women's Institutes in Cambridgeshire have worked together to provide the material for this book. The Cambridge Federation, The Isle of Ely Federation and Huntingdon and Peterborough Federation would like to thank all their members and friends who have worked so hard collecting the information and drawings for this book. Also a special thank you to Eileen Webster who co-ordinated the whole project.

Thanks are also due to everyone who contributed to the updating and revisions for this new expanded edition, including the various co-ordinators who gathered in all the information and those members who wrote fresh entries and provided extra illustrations for the book.

County of
CAMBRIDGESHIRE

Barnack

ᵒWISBECH

R. Nene

PETERBOROUGH

· Benwick

RAMSEY
ᵒ

ELY
ᵒ

R. Ouse

HUNTINGDON
ᵒ

Grafham
Water

GODMANCHESTER
ᵒ

Offord Cluny

· Landbeach

R. Cam

· Great
Wilbrahim

CAMBRIDGE

N

Hildersham
·

Thriplow

ROYSTON

All Saints' church, Castle Camps

🍁 ABBOTSLEY

Abbotsley is situated in what was the old county of Huntingdonshire, sixteen miles west of Cambridge, four miles east of St Neots on the road leading to Great Gransden. The main group of old thatched and tiled houses and cottages still clusters around the 13th century church, dedicated to St Margaret of Antioch, which stands at the highest point in the village. There are more modern homes, some of which radiate outwards to the six farms which form the village boundaries. The parish comprises 1,104 acres of rolling arable farmland interspersed with coppices of mainly deciduous trees and has a population of about 430.

There are two pubs, the Eight Bells and the Jolly Abbot, which both offer good food. The old Victorian school, which today serves as the village hall, is in constant use for community activities, including Mums and Tots and the WI. A full annual programme of events is organised by the Village Hall Committee.

An interesting and unusual feature of the church is the tower, the parapet of which is decorated with a stone figure at each corner. Traditionally, these figures are said to represent William the Conqueror, Harold, Macbeth and Malcolm III. The latter two Kings of Scotland reflect the fact that in the 12th and 13th centuries, as a result of marriage, the Scottish monarch was also the Earl of Huntingdon. The clock, recently restored, dates to the early 1600s. In the churchyard is the fine tabletop tomb of William Heylock, who died in 1688. He left 'unto the poor of Abbotsley £5 of current English money . . . to be paid by my executor . . . to be paid every year.' It still is.

The four kings are also to be seen on the village's hand-carved wooden sign. Other attractions of this lovely village include the duck pond, the children's playing field and High Green, which is the site of the village fete celebrating St Margaret's Day, on the Saturday closest to 20th July.

Tournaments at national level take place at the spectacular

Abbotsley golf complex, with its own hotel and restaurant, owned by Vivien Saunders MBE, the champion professional golfer.

☘ THE ABINGTONS

The Abingtons are delightful villages about eight miles south east of Cambridge. Great and Little Abington are separated by the river Granta, but for social activities they are as one. The name Abington comes from an old Saxon name, Abba.

They each have a fine church dating from the 13th century, both in good condition. There is also a United Reformed church.

Mr Lewis, the schoolmaster until the Second World War, encouraged cricket and rifle shooting in the village. Cricket is still played with a very active club. The rifle club, however, closed in the 1980s. There is a large recreation ground which has football pitches and these are well used in the winter season, the Village Institute providing good pavilion facilities. These facilities are also used by the cricket club in the summer. There is a children's play area in one corner of the recreation ground.

The village still enjoys having celebrations in the cricket meadow for major events. In the past these have been: peace celebrations in 1919 and 1945, the coronations of 1911, 1937 and 1953 and the Queen's Silver Jubilee.

In the Second World War the village played its part by having a canteen in the Village Institute and the army was based at Abington Hall.

The year 1936 saw the development of a Land Settlement Association, a scheme by the government to assist miners from the north unemployed through the Great Depression years. This has now been closed and the holdings sold, some of them being used for small business enterprises. The village has gradually developed into a commuter area for Cambridge and London, although The Welding Institute, or TWI as it is now called, continues to employ a number of local people. A large new Science Park is being developed on their land.

The Abingtons still have a good general store with a post office, a pottery shop which includes a coffee shop, and two garages, one with a café. The village pub, the Three Tuns, is a typical oak beamed hostelry, which enjoys local custom as well as visiting trade. There is a tack shop for the many horse owners in the village, and a kennels. Farmed land surrounds the village, which is a very pleasant place now that the busy A11 road to Norwich bypasses on the western side. Housing development in recent years has been carefully planned so that the village retains its community atmosphere, and the school remains at its heart.

🍁 ALCONBURY & ALCONBURY WESTON

The Alconburys are situated north west of Huntingdon. These two attractive villages are surrounded by arable farmland. Although physically one mile separates the two villages both communities participate in the various activities and services.

The name Alconbury has become well known around the country thanks to the air base. Built in 1938, this was formerly an RAF base but until recently was occupied by the American Air Force.

But there are many more interesting points to the twin villages of Alconbury and Alconbury Weston, including the many fords and bridges which cross Alconbury Brook as it winds its way through the countryside.

In particular, there are two historic bridges worthy of note. Both are built of ashlar, square hewn blocks of stone, and Alconbury Weston bridge incorporates materials alleged to have come from Coppingford church. Described as a medieval platform bridge, it consists of a central pier and two abutments of ashlar. Its modern timber upper structure was washed away by the floods of Easter 1998.

Alconbury bridge, not far from the parish church, has been

9

repaired in recent times with brick parapets, but is believed to date from the 15th century. The interesting design comprises four spans with segmental-pointed arches, chamfered on the face and with cut-water piers. The easternmost arch has been re-built and is semi-circular; other similar repairs have also been carried out.

Although the village is close to the recently upgraded A1 and the A14, and is therefore ideal for rapid cross-country communications, residents enjoy a natural rural environment. The green forms an attractive central feature, and the brook passing through is often lively with ducks and geese.

The Alconburys share the fine 13th century church of St Peter and St Paul. The west tower has a broach spire and inside are fragments of wall paintings and medieval glass. The church is a very beautiful building and has been a witness to the Christian faith for over 700 years!

The modern Alconburys have a population of around 2,000. Although many are employed locally, some commute to other areas.

The villages have good facilities including a junior school, pubs, shops, post offices, C of E and Methodist churches, motor repair garages, a refuse tip with recycling facilities and a surgery with pharmacy and a community nurse. Sport within the villages is centred at the Sports & Social Club which is situated midway between them.

🍁 ALWALTON

Situated five miles south west of the expanding cathedral city of Peterborough, this conservation village is bounded to the west by the A1(M), to the south by the A605 Oundle road and to the north by the Nene valley, which provides attractive walks either across the valley to Castor or through Lynchwood to Ferry Meadow, an extensive country park. Through the valley, from Wansford to Peterborough, runs the Nene Valley Steam Railway, a popular summer attraction.

Alwalton is the home of the East of England Agricultural Society which stages one of the most prestigious agricultural shows in the country. It also hosts the National Shire Horse Society Show in March, and numerous other events.

The focal point of this village is its fine Norman church of St Andrew, started in the 12th century and extensively restored between 1961 and 1966 by the beneficence of Canon The Rev Dr Grimes DD (a former civil engineer), the then parish priest. The other notable buildings are Georgian Alwalton Hall, the Jacobean Manor Farm and the Old Rectory. In addition there are numerous old cottages, some thatched.

The old Victorian School opened in 1846, but through falling rolls closed in 1981, eventually being acquired by a local chartered civil engineer, who whilst preserving all its original features sympathetically converted it for professional office use.

The local hostelry, the Wheatsheaf Inn, is another old building, and close by is the tiny post office/village store and the old blacksmith's (now a private house). The village hall was erected in memory of Colonel Dane, who formerly resided in Alwalton Hall. During 1998 this was demolished and rebuilt, to be reopened on 26th September 1998 by Sir Philip Naylor-Leyland of Milton Estate, a descendant of Colonel Dane's wife.

The village was the birthplace of the famous Frederick Henry Royce, born 27th March 1863, the youngest of the five children of James and Mary Royce. He lived there for only the first four years of his life, moving with his father to London, but returned to Peterborough aged 14 to take up an apprenticeship at the Great Northern Railway Works. He subsequently became an electrical engineer, with a partner forming F.H. Royce & Co in 1884. After some years of struggle he built the first Royce 10 horsepower car in 1903/1904, before becoming co-founder of Rolls Royce. There is a plaque to his memory in St Andrew's church.

Another notable resident for a time, to whom there is also a plaque in the church, was Francis Arthur Perkins, the founder of

11

Perkins Engines, world famous for its diesel engines. He lived in the Hall prior to his death on 15th October 1967 and he and his wife are interred in St Andrew's churchyard.

🍁 BABRAHAM

Babraham was one of the important ancient settlements in this part of the county, situated as it is at the foot of those crucial defence posts the Gog Magog hills. Two very ancient highways are close by: the Icknield Way, a prehistoric trade route which runs by Bourn Bridge, and Via Devana, the old 'Worsted Road' which runs along the Worsted Dyke by the northern edge of the settlement. It is thought too that the street which passes the Madeline Hall, continuing across the main road and through the chalky hill to Worsted Lodge, is very old.

In 1575 Babraham was owned by Robert Taylor who built himself a very fine house in almost the same position as the present hall. This was described as one of the first Gothic houses in the country. In 1593 Horatio Palacicini, a Genoese adventurer, became the owner. He had been a political agent for Mary Tudor and after her death changed his religion and became money lender to Elizabeth I. He commanded an English man-of-war during the Armada.

Babraham Hall was built by the Adeane family in 1833–37, replacing at least three other houses which have stood on this site. The family remained here until the house was sold to the Agricultural Research Council in 1948, although they continued to own most of the land in the village, which was subsequently sold on the death of Sir Robert Adeane. His daughter and grandson still have houses in the village.

In the Middle Ages this was a wealthy place, being assessed higher than any other village in the Chilford Hundred excepting Linton. Babraham had an open system of fields, varying in number from four to six. The open fields were enclosed during the period 1794–1829 without a formal agreement as almost all the land was in the possession of the owner. This fact has enabled more advanced methods of farming to be employed here than elsewhere. Most important was the breeding of both sheep and cattle by Jonas Webb, tenant of Church Farm. He acquired a worldwide reputation for his achievements. A statue of him bought by subscription from his 'Friends in Many Lands' stands in the village street; this formerly stood in the Corn Exchange in Cambridge.

The church dedicated to St Peter is a very fine building, the earliest part of which is an impressive tower dating from the 12th century. The chancel dates from the mid 13th century and the nave and aisles from the 15th. There were at one time five bells but only one now remains.

In the centre of the village opposite the George Inn is a row of almshouses with the old schoolhouse in the middle. The school was established under the will of Judith Benet though there had been a schoolmaster in the village as early as 1607. The school provided free education for the local children and was in use as a primary school until a new one was built opposite the vicarage in 1959.

Next to the George on one side stands the oldest house in the village, Chalk Farmhouse. On the other side is a row of Victorian farmworkers' cottages, now much improved from the days when the tenants had to fetch their water from a pump outside the inn.

🍁 BALSHAM

The village of Balsham, in the very south east corner of Cambridgeshire, is an old (pre-Domesday) and thriving village, originally agricultural and completely self sufficient. The village has changed with the population trends, dropping in numbers as agriculture dwindled and people moved out of the countryside into the cities, but now has doubled again in size to last century's level. Current population is around 1,570 with approximately 600 houses. It may expand further in accordance with Cambridgeshire Structure Plan.

Electricity did not reach here until 1949 and sewerage not for another 14 years and there is no gas. Balsham is classed as a 'larger village', having the local junior school, post office and stores, butcher and dairy with local deliveries. Farming is still important and there is a small company making steel framed buildings. In addition, many small businesses are run from the village, including small-works builders, electricians, hairdressers and there is also a computer consultant, chiropodist, dressmaker, floral artist and landscape gardener.

The 1990s saw the closure of all but two shops and the loss of the village garage, a builder and builder's merchant, an agricultural supply company and a public house. Two local family farms have also ceased their function. At the same time there has been considerable building of new houses, mostly of executive type, but also some smaller and cheaper dwellings to enable the young to stay in the village. A sizeable proportion of the working population commutes to Cambridge and its environs or to other nearby towns, all made easier by the opening of the nearby Charterhouse bridge over the A11 London-Norwich trunk road. Some commuting to London and its surrounding area takes place via Audley End train station or by the greatly improved A11 and M11 road links.

Balsham is an active community and boasts many societies. A biennial flower festival is held in the church and there is a Cross Country Horse Ride every autumn, in conjunction with the neighbouring Hildersham parish, which draws entrants from a very wide radius. One of the village's more unusual events is the Plough Monday celebration. On the second Monday in the New Year a dozen or so old ploughmen (or similar nowadays!) haul a hand plough around the houses and two pubs collecting for charity. Those who do not contribute traditionally have their lawns ploughed through!

There are still many old and noteworthy properties in the village, a lot of them thatched, and there are 36 Grade II listed buildings. The church of Holy Trinity is said to have been defended by Balsham's last survivor against the invading Danish hordes in the early 11th century, a heroic feat commemorated in the village sign. The centre of the village was designated a conservation area in 1995.

❧ BAR HILL

Bar Hill, a new village created in the middle of farmland, came into being at the suggestion of the Cambridgeshire County Council, as an alternative to ribbon development. It lies seven miles to the north west of Cambridge, just off the old Roman road of Via Devana, now known as the A14.

The first intimation of a new parish came to the inhabitants of Dry Drayton in 1948. It was given ministerial approval in 1964 and 350 acres of land in the parish of Dry Drayton were acquired. There was opposition to the plan, including some from the nearby National Institute of Agricultural Botany, who feared that pollen from gardens would seriously affect their experiments, hence the original ban on growing any member of the cruciferous group of plants. The ground had previously grown fruit for Chivers at Histon.

The new parish was planned around a large village green, with school, village hall and church bordering on it. An area apart from these was set aside for industrial development and shops. The Radburn Principle developed by Clarence Stein and Henry Wright at Radburn, New Jersey was adopted and pedestrian and vehicular traffic are separated as much as possible. A road encircles the village with a number of cul-de-sacs leading to the centre, so that the main facilities are within easy walking distance of all parts of the village. This also allows for small communities within the main residential part with safe areas for children to play. Unfortunately, not all the excellent facilities planned were carried out. At first the project did not succeed, but a few hardy pioneers persisted and now it has become a success story.

15

The village has adopted as its logo the great bustard, a bird which formerly lived here but is now extinct in this country.

Before the Dissolution of the Monasteries the land belonged to Crowland or Croyland Abbey in Lincolnshire. The abbot had authority to hang thieves caught red-handed. At least 12 skeletons were discovered at Galles Piece near the Dry Drayton/Oakington crossroads during roadworks. One abbot is said to have hanged a man for stealing 16 eggs, although this was not on his land.

Another discovery was a Saxon drinking vessel which is now in the Fitzwilliam Museum in Cambridge. For a period the land belonged to the Cutts family who lived at Childerley or Cildersley, later it was bought by the Duke of Bedford whose main purpose was to create a park. Some of the old field names are retained. Thruffles is a corruption of 'three furrows', so called because the nature of the ground made it necessary to plough it three different ways.

There are now over 5,000 residents and in 1997 Bar Hill celebrated 30 years since its formation. Many and varied groups use the primary school including carpet bowls and judo clubs and the village has its own library, opened about 1990. The original church was outgrown and a new building was consecrated in 1991.

🍁 BARNACK

Barnack has been described as a village that has 'grown from its own earth'. Almost the entire village is built on land from which stone was quarried from Roman times to the 16th century, and the 'ragstone' has been used for important buildings throughout East Anglia, including the abbeys of Crowland, Ramsey and Bury St Edmunds and Peterborough and Ely cathedrals.

The village lies just off the Roman Ermine Street and the first mentioned record of Barnack is in the *Anglo-Saxon Chronicle* of the 9th century where it is spelled Beonica.

The church, which is built of Barnack ragstone, is of great

Kingsley House at Barnack

interest. Among its notable features are the Saxon tower dating from 1020 with a broach spire added around 1200. In the north aisle there is a perfectly preserved 10th century Anglo-Saxon sculpture of Christ in Majesty and a fine 13th century font.

In 1976 a National Nature Reserve was created on the 22 hectares of the old quarry workings. These hummocky spoil tips, known as the 'Hills and Holes', contain a variety of rare plants characteristic of limestone soils. Barnack is one of the two richest sites in Britain for the beautiful pasque flower and the grasslands also support a wealth of vetches, cowslips and rare orchids.

In 1965 a new estate built on the former parkland of Kingsley House won a Civic Trust Award for its successful blending into the heart of the village.

In 1796 the stone building situated in School Lane was built by the 1st Marquis of Exeter for 140 children. It was leased to the

National Society for the Education of the Poor. A new infant room was added by the rector in 1896. This stone building is now Barnack village hall, known as the Wilfrid Wood Hall. The present school was officially opened in 1951.

Among many old and interesting buildings in the parish are two houses of special note. One is the former rectory built in the 14th century and now known as Kingsley House. It was here that Charles Kingsley, the novelist, spent his childhood during his father's ministry. The second house, standing two miles from the village, is Burghley House. William Cecil, later Lord Burghley (Lord Treasurer to Queen Elizabeth I), acquired the manor of Barnack and built the magnificent palace in the latter half of the 16th century. Burghley House is still occupied by the Cecil family.

🍁 BARRINGTON

Barrington is situated eight miles south of Cambridge, with a population of about 1,000. The village is most attractive with its large expanse of green consisting of some 23 acres and the mile long street running through the centre. Old thatched cottages and new houses blend together around the edge of the green. Many years ago villagers who owned cows and horses would pay ten shillings per year for grazing rights, whereas goats and geese could graze free of charge. Some feel it is a pity this no longer takes place, as the cattle seemed to give added charm to the village scene.

The church is dedicated to All Saints, under which name it is mentioned in 1400. It is quite big and is said to have been built with the chalk, or 'clunch', from the local pit on the outskirts of the village. Barrington is dominated by two tall chimneys puffing their white smoke across the sky. They belong to Rugby Portland Cement Company and cement has been produced there since 1900. The cement is despatched by road or by a light railway that is linked to the main line at Foxton. Many years ago when boys left school they either went into the cement factory or on the farms to work as there was so little choice. Arable farming goes on today, but there are no dairy farms now.

The Church of England primary school and schoolhouse were built in 1838 and the roofs are thatched in Tudor style. A tradition of the school was to celebrate May Day each year with dancing around the maypole either in the school playground or on the village green. A May Queen and her attendants would be chosen, and the boys would carry staves decorated with flowers while the girls would carry garlands, all made at home with help from their mothers. Prizes would be awarded for the best display. This tradition was discontinued in the 1960s.

The windmill standing south of the green was also built with clunch in 1822 and stood derelict for many years until it was renovated and converted into a modern home (minus sails of course).

The river Rhee flows through the parish and in medieval days was said to be the boundary between Mercia and East Anglia. Bulbeck Mill stands along the river bank and acquired the name in about the year 1240. It is no longer a working mill but thrives as the Barrington factory of Grant Instruments, makers of scientific instruments.

A character often remembered by older parishioners was Fred Patman. On Rogation Sunday he would don top hat and tails, and, complete with handbell and sword, would 'Beat the Bounds' and walk along the Roman road to the 'Old Guildhall'.

🍁 BARTON

Barton is a village of approximately 820 inhabitants situated three miles south west of Cambridge. It was a flourishing village in Saxon times and is mentioned in the Domesday Book, with a population of 31, growing to 425 in 1279. At Lord's bridge, near an old ford across the Bourn Brook, cremation urns and amphorae were discovered in the 19th century and iron slave chains and fire-dogs came from the same area. They are now housed in the Cambridge Museum of Archaeology.

The village itself was built around a green just west of the church. Bird's Farm, originally a late medieval hall, is the earliest surviving house in the village. St Peter's church dates back to the 12th century but the style of the present building is pure 14th century. It was probably at the time of William Dowsing that the wall paintings, which since 1320 had covered the entire walls of the nave, were concealed under whitewash. In 1929 they were restored to view, and in 1980 a five-year programme of conservation was introduced. The 14th century screen and the pulpit bearing the date 1635 are much admired. The church has six bells; the sixth one was installed in October 1998.

There are two public houses, the Hoops and the White Horse. The latter used to brew its own beer on the premises. When it was owned by three elderly ladies they displayed a sign: 'No Swearing'.

An annual event in the past was the Village Feast with stalls in School Lane and Hoops Yard. Today a Horticultural Show is held in July, when many of the village groups are involved.

The recreation ground has a bowling green and two hard tennis courts. There is also a children's play area. The village has a football team and in the years past there was a cricket team and a tug-of-war team. Alongside the recreation ground there is a strip of grassland about a quarter of a mile long, known as The Leys, pronounced 'lays', which, over the years, has become common ground. In years past it was used as an archery ground.

Burwash Manor Farm, an early 17th century farmhouse, timber-framed and plastered, contains a Jacobean plastered ceiling and fireplace. The house lies within a two-armed moat of the same date. Today Burwash Barns house many and varied shops and a tea room.

Barton is very fortunate in having its own village school, a post office within the village shop, the specialist shoe shop 'Carters' and a petrol station. Several houses in the village offer bed and breakfast.

Barton village sign

Situated on the outskirts of Barton is the Mullard Radio Astronomy Observatory. The Cambridge University radio telescopes have been built along the line of the old Cambridge to Bedford railway.

The Ministry of Defence Rifle Range is on the outskirts of the village and nearby are the kennels of the Trinity Foot Beagles.

🍁 BASSINGBOURN-CUM-KNEESWORTH

Bassingbourn is an Anglo-Saxon name and the first settlement was probably in the Bowling Alley area, which is situated beside the brook.

John of Gaunt owned a castle at the north end of the village – a public house near the site of the castle was named after him. Years ago it was converted into a private house, and still has the same name. It is reported that Oliver Cromwell's mother resided in the house known as Church Farm.

The parish church, St Peter and St Paul, situated in North End was built in 1272. The chancel was erected in the middle of the 14th century. The Congregational church which is in the recreation ground (formerly known as Meeting Close) was built in 1791. In 1982 the church was condemned as unsafe, and services are now held in a small building in South End.

In 1840 the notorious case of the unburied child commenced. The infant, Jane Rumbold, born 12th December 1839, was baptised by the Non-conformist minister, C. Moase, on 8th February 1840 and died on 14th February 1840. Application was made to the vicar Reverend W. H. Chapman, for interment in the churchyard; the vicar refused to bury the child – he said he would not bury any child that was baptised at the Meeting. Five times the body of Jane Rumbold was taken to the churchyard. Eventually a High Court judge declared the baptism valid, and the vicar lost the case after five years' litigation. The child had been kept in the house, a recess being made in an empty chimney to preserve the body – the corpse had been taken to and from church so many times that a second coffin had to be made. The vicar still would not perform the service, but the vicar of Whaddon, the Reverend W. Coulcher, buried the child on 30th January 1845. On a bitterly cold, wintry day, snow fell fast. Notwithstanding, the people turned out in crowds to hear the bell tolled and to witness the burial of the child by the side of her mother and ten of her brothers and sisters in the Parish churchyard.

About 1850 a Cambridge professor discovered coprolites here. The excavation of these fossil phosphates provided a prosperous industry over the latter half of the century during which time the population almost doubled; much labour was imported and this led to vagrancy in the locality. Coprolites were dug by hand, washed, loaded and carted to Royston station.

Straw plaiting, a part-time industry, was carried on by women in their houses – this found favour for a considerable time. The straw plait was sewn onto bonnets and hats modelled on stone moulds. Some of these moulds are still in the village.

In the first decade of the 20th century there were about 1,200 inhabitants, now there are 3,500. At one time there were 14 shops in Bassingbourn and one in Kneesworth. There are now six shops in Bassingbourn and one in Kneesworth. There were twelve public houses in Bassingbourn and two in Kneesworth. There are now two in each location.

A famous inhabitant lived at Kneesworth Hall in the early part of this century. He was Lord Knutsford, the second Viscount. Before he succeeded to the title he was the Honourable Sydney Holland. At this time he was appointed Chairman of the London Hospital in Whitechapel, where some of the wards are named the Holland Wards. Not only in London but in Bassingbourn and Kneesworth he showed his care for others. He saw the need for a District Nurse, and brought one from the London Hospital and paid her out of his own pocket. When village people needed urgent hospital treatment he arranged for them to be admitted to the London and paid their fare, or took them in his own carriage. He built and equipped a village hall in Kneesworth and was a member of the local cricket club. When Sir Peter Scott was a small boy he spent long periods at Kneesworth Hall as Lord Knutsford was his guardian.

In 1936 the Air Ministry acquired nearly 500 acres of arable land in Bassingbourn and nearby Wendy for the erection of an aerodrome. This provided employment for many people in the locality. During the Second World War it was a Bomber Station and many bombing raids were carried out over enemy targets by pilots stationed there. The base is now a barracks for training soldiers.

🍁 BENWICK

Benwick is a unique fen village, being built on a rodden, but drainage has caused the peat to shrink and the rodden to be lowered, and this

Benwick village

has caused buildings to tip and crack, until they finally either fell down or were pulled down.

This means there are few really old buildings standing, the main one remaining being the village school which was built in 1873. The Wesleyan chapel built in 1833 does still stand, although the walls and floors are tilting. The Baptist chapel built in 1818 was pulled down in the 1960s, and St Mary's church built in 1850 was pulled down in 1985. However, other churches received some benefit from this, as stained glass windows went to Doddington church, the font and the door to St Jude's church in Peterborough, and the clock was sent to March Museum.

Once all the inhabitants (apart from the schoolmaster, the rector, the village policeman and the sub-postmaster) earned their living from the land. In 1899 it was noted that a boy was absent from school for 'cow-tending', and children were continually absent to work on the land at potato-picking time and gleaning. It seems that

BLUNTISHAM 🍁

the only fun they had was to take time off for a Band of Hope Demonstration or picnics and Sunday School festivals, for Plough Monday or the Village Feast in July, and they were late for school on May 1st 'through being out with garlands'!

There were seven public houses in the High Street, but now only one remains, namely the Five Alls, standing for 'I govern all (the Queen), I plea for all (lawyer), I pray for all (parson), I fight for all (soldier) and I pay for all (working man)'.

During the Second World War there was a dummy aerodrome in the village, which used to trick enemy aircraft into thinking they were over an RAF camp or the marshalling yards at March. More bombs dropped at Benwick than anywhere else in the county, sending London evacuees scuttling home because they felt safer there!

It is true that the face of Benwick is changing. The damp, low cottages are being replaced with smart, centrally-heated homes. When asked why they choose to move to Benwick newcomers answer that it is for the peace and quiet, and that once they see the sign 'Benwick', they know they are out of the rat-race once more.

🍁 BLUNTISHAM

Bluntisham is situated four miles east of St Ives. It was part of the old county of Huntingdonshire. This village has a very long history. The prehistoric occupation of this area is suggested by the discovery of flint tools. Romans too, used this site, leaving pottery vessels and a bronze statue (now housed in the British Museum).

At the junction of Rectory Road and the High Street, standing on the corner, is Bluntisham House, once the rectory. It stands well back with lawns, flower beds and thickets sloping down to the road. The house has a Georgian front with a rather ornate stone doorway taken from the Old Slepe Hall in St Ives. It looks a suitable setting for one of the detective stories written by one of its former occupants – Dorothy

L. Sayers, whose father was rector here for some years.

In the High Street is the picturesque Rectory Cottage, with timber framed gable end and typical Huntingdonshire mansard roof. Beyond this is the old village school, now used by the play group. Opposite is the Nonconformist Meeting House and its Sunday school, where Belgian refugees were housed in the First World War. Just to the right of the chapel is Meeting Walk, now a pleasant footpath through the centre of the village. It is said to have originated from the special path used to take coffins to the churchyard for burial, avoiding, as far as possible, inhabited or frequented parts of the parish on which the passing corpse might bring bad luck.

The home of the Tebbutt family for about 150 years was called Walnut Trees after the two trees which stood opposite. Outside on the wall of the house was an elaborate sign which was made by Pittoors, an ornamental ironworker, who with his wife and four sons were refugees from Belgium during the First World War. He was provided with a small forge and a supply of Swedish iron. This craftsman produced beautiful work, the sale of which helped to keep him and his family.

Mill Lane was the site of the mill from 1608 to 1899. It had a dark tradition connected to the old mill of long ago and a ghost was said to be seen. The last miller would not stay in the mill at night on his own. Now on certain nights it is said the sound of the wind in the sails can still be heard.

St Mary's church was first started in 1330, with the chancel and north chapel or vestry. Various monies had been left for the teaching of the poor of the whole parish and a room under the church tower and was used as a schoolroom. The church is said to sit on the boundary of Bluntisham and Earith.

A curious local custom existed whereby a bride could free herself of all debts incurred before her marriage, by walking across the road naked to her husband's house!

🍁 BOTTISHAM

Bottisham is very much a 'fen-edge' village, built along the line of a small ridge, slightly higher than the surrounding fens, thus making the village long and fairly narrow. The parish church is only 51 feet above the sea level. In more recent times, land on which some of the village is built was owned by St Bartholomew's Hospital and two cast iron posts in the garden of Parsonage Farm record this fact.

The village contains some notable old houses: Stocks – once a village shop and now a restaurant – Tudor House, Bottisham Place, the old Court House and an unusual group of cottages called The Arch. The Grange, which now serves as a private residential home for the elderly, was the vicarage and Bleak House was used for a time as a private school. The 13th century church of Holy Trinity is said by Pevsner to be 'one of the most interesting churches in Cambridgeshire'.

Judging by reminiscences, even in the hard times of the 1920s and 1930s, life was never dull. Harry Morgan and Alfred Arber, schoolmaster and parish clerk respectively, dispensed discipline in their spheres and earned the affection of generations and have passed into village folklore. Perhaps the geographical location, midway between Cambridge and Newmarket with their two contrasting cultures, gave the village its vitality.

The vast change, within a lifetime, from a rural community of about 700 to the present 2,000 or more seems to have been caused by a series of friendly 'invasions'. Each one has added to the enormous range of occupations, interests and talents which is now enjoyed.

The first was educational, when in 1937 the second Village College in the county was built. It was one of the Countrymen's Colleges as envisaged by Henry Morris. When it opened it served as a centre for 11 villages with a population totalling 7,000 as a school in the daytime and as a 'University' and social centre in the evenings when parents attended.

27

The wartime invaders were the Tank Corps, the RAF, evacuees and finally 1,800 Americans. Some of each group formed lasting ties with the village people.

The post-war building boom introduced new faces with each small development until the large Park Estate brought a flood of newcomers – almost literally, as they stepped straight into a world of mud and wellies, because of the reluctance to make up the roads. As the number of residents grew more shops opened, better medical services were necessary and a new Family Practitioner Group Practice, including a baby clinic, was built. A playgroup and nursery school opened, a separate primary school was built and more recently a large indoor swimming pool and sports centre have been added to the amenities available in the village. Gradually the old and the new have emerged to make a village well provided for and acting as a centre for the surrounding smaller villages.

The village can claim a distinguished 'first'. MAGPAS – the local flying doctor service – was the brainchild of Dr Silverston MBE who practised here for many years.

🍁 BOXWORTH

A 'small well wooded village' has been an apt description of Boxworth since the earliest records of 1086, when it was spelt Bochesworde.

The important building is St Peter's church, of early Norman origin, which once had a spire, destroyed in a gale and replaced by a castellated tower. Two famous scholars are associated with it. John Bois (Boyce) was rector here from 1595 to 1637 and translated the Apocrypha for the King James version of the Bible. He died in 1643 aged 83 and was buried at Ely.

By the altar is the burial stone of Nicholas Saunderson FRS, blind from birth but who became Professor of Mathematics at Cambridge University. His horse took him to Cambridge and back to Boxworth each day.

The outline of the old medieval village can be seen in fields near the church, as hollow ways, 'ridge and furrow' ploughing, crop marks etc. Overhall Wood with the remains of its old manor and moat is well known for its oxslips and bluebells, its bird life and badger colonies. In the woods in Boxworth live wild deer, such as muntjac and roedeer.

The Boxworth Experimental Husbandry Farm (ADAS) of great renown is to be found in Battlegate Road. This gives employment to some of the villagers, others being employed on local farms. A small number commute to Cambridge.

The oldest family in Boxworth is that of the Thornhills. They bought large estates in 1785 and Edmund Henry Thornhill came to live in the manor house in 1884. The last member of the family to live there was Lt Col E.B. Thornhill MC, DL, who died in April 1998 aged 100 years. The present lord of the manor and patron of the church living is his son George Edmund Peter Thornhill of Newark.

Old documents relating to Boxworth from the 13th century onward have been transcribed and collected in book form to be seen in the County Records Office, the University Library and the Society of Antiquaries in London. Extracts are available in the church or at Church Farm. Village 'bygones' have also been assembled at Church Farm. These include the old bakery dough trough and old farm implements, as well as Victorian domestic items and clothing.

🍁 BRAMPTON

Situated now within the triangle formed by the A1, the A14 and the A141, Brampton was mentioned in the Domesday Book. The name is a corruption of Brantune, a place of bramble bushes. Its population has grown from 780 in 1801 to 5,220 in 1997.

The Manor of Brampton was one of the Royal residences. Brampton Wood, to the west of the village, is one of the few remaining areas of the Forest of Wabridge which at one time stretched from Stamford, Lincolnshire in the north down to Oxfordshire. There was excellent hunting. The Manor ceased to be a private residence in the early 1960s and became the Cheshire Home for Cambridgeshire and Bedfordshire.

The parish church stands guard at the east end of Brampton, a fine building, parts of which date from the early 14th century. Local 'notables' are buried here – the Earls of Sandwich, Brigadier General Robert Bernard Sparrow and his wife Lady Olivia Bernard Sparrow, a great benefactress to the village. She founded the school, the Round House, built as an infirmary, octagonal in shape because for reasons of economy there was one central fire to heat the six two-bedded rooms. She purchased a property to be used for the education of girls in the parish and also built a number of cottages for farm labourers and their families.

There are a few listed buildings but the only one with a claim to fame is Pepys House. It was at one time owned by a relative of Samuel Pepys' family, and the diarist himself lived there for a time and often visited in later years.

One of his favourite haunts was the Black Bull, a coaching inn and the oldest in Brampton. Of the twelve known to have existed, only four remain; of the rest, five have ceased trading within living memory although happily two have survived as private residences.

The main occupation in the area was formerly farming although in the 1920s and 1930s there was a large nursery which supplied rose bushes world-wide and in one particular year a quarter of a million bushes were sent to local authorities in Canada. The rambler *Dorothy Perkins* was bred here.

There has been an RAF presence in Brampton since 1940 although the station was not permanently established until 1957, and this is now a major employer. Its establishment as well as the improved road and rail links with London have played a part in the residential development of Brampton.

🍁 BROUGHTON

Broughton, which means settlement on the brook, is a small, attractive village nestling in a hollow, surrounded by fields and situated in an ideal position for the towns of Ramsey, St Ives and Huntingdon.

In the 12th century it was an important meeting place for the Abbots of Ramsey who held their Courts of Justice at Broughton Castle. It is thought the castle was demolished at the time of the Reformation and only a moat remains today.

Interesting features around the village are an Elizabethan rectory, a 17th century farmhouse with Dutch gables which was built at the time of the drainage of the fens, and on the village green a small early 19th century lock-up.

The 11th century church with its impressive spire holds central position in the village. It has four bells, a Norman font and over the chancel arch is a finely preserved medieval wall painting of the Doom. On the south wall of the nave are paintings of the expulsion of Adam and Eve from the Garden of Eden.

Also in the village is a Baptist chapel erected by Benjamin How senior in 1861. The village school built in 1842 is now in use as a village hall.

Among the more modern buildings, which include a very useful sub post office, there are still a number of 16th century farmhouses, several old thatched cottages and a country pub. In the past agriculture, including a village dairy, was the main industry. Another important local family business was that of the wheelwright, carpenter and undertaker. Some of these are depicted in the hand-carved oak village sign on the green. The annual Rogation walk, an old Christian tradition of village life, is still practised today.

The village maintains a lively community spirit with many social activities, one popular attraction being the Broughton Flower

Festival which the church stages every two years.

🍁 BUCKDEN

Buckden, a thriving and historic village located 60 miles from London on the Great North Road, was originally known as Bugedene. It is listed in the Domesday survey of 1086 as a manor belonging to the Bishop of Lincoln, consisting of a church, a mill, a few cottages and a wood a mile square, the whole being valued at £16.10s.

For seven and a half centuries successive Bishops of Lincoln had their principal residence at Buckden Palace, now known as Buckden Towers. The 15th century Great Tower and Inner Gatehouse were completed under Bishop Russell's episcopacy in 1480. During 1533–34 Catherine of Aragon was imprisoned here before being removed to Kimbolton. In 1957, when the building and grounds were in sad neglect, ownership passed to the Claretian Missionaries. Under their care, the Catholic church of St Hugh of Lincoln was built in 1959. Subsequently, the buildings and grounds have been restored to retain their historic interest and adapt them to modern requirements for religious, educational and social activities.

Adjoining the Towers is the impressive parish church of St Mary. The chancel and porch are 13th century and the nave 15th century. During the tumultuous time of Cromwell, the rood and most of the stained glass were removed. The main door still hangs on its original hinges, as every latecomer can testify!

Buckden Methodist church, built in 1876, was refurbished and modernised in 1986. Its Sunday school building, completed in 1911, provides a venue for many church and local groups.

The three village churches combine to form an ecumenical movement and it was this group that started *The Buckden Roundabout*, the village's monthly magazine which is distributed free to every house.

Buckden has several fine 16th and 17th century houses and many modern houses have greatly extended the village in recent years. There are two sets of almshouses in Church Street, supported by local charities.

Coaching inns have played a large part in the history of the village and the 16th century Lion and 18th century George are still as popular today with travellers and with local people. Public houses used to abound, but now only the Vine and the Spread Eagle remain.

The population of Buckden parish has now reached some 3,500, with a primary school of 400 pupils. The village is also fortunate to have a doctors' surgery, a library, and a variety of quality shops. The village hall has been greatly improved and extended and there is a recreation ground with children's play area, together with facilities for cricket, football, tennis and bowls. On the nearby river Ouse there is an extensive marina with leisure facilities.

Buckden is proud of its historic past, but has not hesitated to move with the times and today provides its inhabitants with a varied but still essentially rural quality of life.

🍁 BURWELL

A large village near the Old Fen, Burwell is located some twelve miles east of Cambridge and four miles north of Newmarket. The population is around 5000 and is expected to grow, as more houses are being built according to a set village plan.

Burwell is two miles long and has two distinct areas, High Street, and North Street and Newnham, which are linked together by the Causeway. North Street and Newnham are former commercial areas associated with water transport on the Lodes. Hythe Lane would have led to the The Hythe which was a loading place for barges.

St Mary's church, a fine 15th century building in the Perpendicular style, stands in the High Street. There is evidence of Norman work in the tower. Extensive restoration has been carried out on this building over the past few years. In the churchyard can be seen the Flaming Heart tombstone marking the burial place of 78 persons who died in a barn fire whilst watching a puppet show on 8th September 1727. It was never fully established whether the fire ignited by accident or was started deliberately by someone who had a grudge against the puppet master. Unfortunately the fire spread rapidly and the doors had been locked to keep out unwanted persons so the loss of life was great.

The site of Burwell Castle adjoins the western side of the churchyard. The castle, started in the 12th century, was famous in the reign of King Stephen, because during a siege the notorious Geoffrey de Mandeville was slain. Only the moat now remains with the spring which filled it, hence the site is known as Spring Close. The Mandeville name lives on in a road behind the church.

There are many old and interesting buildings in the village including the manor house and Maltings Corner in the High Street, a long stone building, The Old Priory, once known as The Parsonage, and the Tunbridge in Low Road.

As well as its agricultural background, Burwell has always been a place of industry; digging of turf (peat), cement making, quarrying clunch for house building and making chemical fertilizers were all carried on in the past. Now agricultural engineers and a factory making corrugated cardboard are among the chief employers, but many people travel to Newmarket or Cambridge to work. At one time the Burwell and District Omnibus Company was run by a local family, but like the railway station which is now extinct, Burwell and District Buses are no longer with us.

A Windmill Trust was set up and has restored an old windmill to working order, and the Museum Trust has converted a barn into a museum for the village.

🍁 BURY

Bury is situated on the very edge of the fens adjacent to Ramsey. It is in an idyllic setting with the lovely church of the Holy Cross, parts of which date from the 12th century, standing on a hill overlooking the babbling brook and the golf course (it is called Ramsey Golf Course although most of it is situated in Bury parish). Bury church has one piece of furniture so special that it has been borrowed by the Royal Academy of Arts for an exhibition. This is a lectern, not in the shape of an eagle like so many, but more box like with a single leg and a stone base, and intricately carved.

The old stone-built two-room school in the High Street is now converted to a dwelling house and the school has moved to a new building in Owls End which has recently had extensions to cater for the extra children brought to the village by more house building. Bury has expanded rapidly since the 1960s and is still growing. There were 496 voters on the electoral roll in 1967 and 1,225 voters in 1997.

Most of the residents' everyday needs can be met within the village by the sub post office, the general stores, the garage and the public house, the White Lion, which also serves meals.

In 1997 a new village hall was officially opened by the then Prime Minister the Rt Hon John Major. It is well used and a valuable asset to the community.

🍁 BYTHORN

At the time of the Domesday Book, Bythorn was in the possession of Ramsey Abbey, with a population of 17 able-bodied men, and was one of the parishes belonging to the Leightonstone Hundred.

This small, picturesque village is situated beside the A14, twelve miles west of Huntingdon. The three roads into it lead to the attractive green in the centre, which is bounded by pleasant houses, the church and the old school. The school closed in 1969, and its building then housed a thriving nursery school for 19 years. The bell still hangs in the tower. On the green are two large pollarded horse chestnut trees that have provided conkers for generations of children.

St Lawrence's church is noted for its lack of a spire. This was removed in 1960 when found to be leaning dangerously and was replaced by a little hexagonal copper cap on a wooden frame. Lack of funds prevented a full restoration.

The village hall, originally a Baptist chapel and with its gravestones remaining, has been refurbished and now hosts many varied events. The other focus of social life is the White Hart. Formerly a coaching inn, it has been extended and altered over the years and now has a noted bar and restaurant.

☘ CASTLE CAMPS

Tucked away in the south east corner of Cambridgeshire, Castle Camps borders onto both Suffolk and Essex, occupying some 3,198 acres. Tranquil rural views of all three counties can be seen from the village. The village name derives from the ancient earthworks and a Norman castle whose moat is still discernible. A Norman church – All Saints – remains near the site of the castle within one of the baileys. It is one of the highest points in Cambridgeshire (a giddy 415 feet above sea level!). The present village is about a mile north of the earlier castle site and one story suggests that the villagers decamped in the 17th century to avoid the worst ravages of the plague, to an area then known as Camps Green, a name that still appears on some maps.

Immediately after his conquest of Britain in 1066, William I divided most of England between his Norman followers. Camps Castle was part of a large estate given to Aubrey de Vere. It was held by his family, the Earls of Oxford, for over 500 years. The family seat was Castle Hedingham, Essex, where the castle was far more magnificent although the motte is a similar size. Legend has it that there was a tunnel from Camps Castle to Hedingham Castle, but evidence is hard to establish. The estate of Castle Camps, used as a residence by the Earls, included a large enclosed park, windmill and fishery. 'Pond Bay' can still be seen on some maps between the church and the present village. No warfare appears to be recorded and it seems that Castle Camps was used mainly as an administrative centre for the many Cambridgeshire estates of the de Vere family. In 1584, Camps Castle was sold to Thomas Skynner, a wealthy London merchant, and passed rapidly through various hands before being given to Charterhouse School in 1611. The manor of Castle Camps remained with Charterhouse until quite recent times when it was purchased by a local farmer.

The parish of Castle Camps, which includes Camps End and Olmstead Green, currently has a population of some 600. It has always been a farming community whose population peaked at about 950 in the 1850s, but unlike today, when many commute, most villagers used to work on the land. Indeed, there are still villagers who can recall the long days of hard toil using horses and the subsequent steam machinery, before the advent of the highly mechanised modern farming of recent decades.

Although only some four miles from Haverhill, Suffolk, Castle Camps is fairly remote, only gaining the telephone in the early 1930s, piped water in 1937 and electricity in 1949. The relative isolation has probably contributed to the close community structure. Its rural tranquillity, itself slowly changing, belies an active community, with branches of most of the common village organisations and the latest asset being a hard-surfaced multi-sports area, initiated by the young people, then financed and constructed in less than nine months. During the Second World War Castle Camps was the site of a busy airfield and in 1994 a memorial was erected in Park Lane at the site of the North Gate.

As with most villages, there are some local legends; an

unidentified soul is said to be interred in Wigmore pond, now filled in, and a ghost is reputed to haunt the area in Homers Lane where a cottage used to stand. It was here in 1850 that a husband and his sister-in-law allegedly murdered his wife by poisoning. They were later convicted and became the last two people to be publicly hanged in Cambridgeshire. In comparatively recently times, workmen carrying out alterations at nearby Shudy Camps Park uncovered a priest's hole which had hitherto remained undiscovered.

All Saints' church, which has recently been restored, has a magnificent nave roof of king posts upon tie beams. On the outside of the south wall of the church can be seen a stone bearing a Latin inscription described as a remarkable elegiac couplet. To many, however, All Saints' church and Castle Camps will always be associated with the rector John Bode, who wrote the hymn *O Jesus I have promised* in the 1960s whilst ministering here and who is buried in the churchyard.

🍁 CASTOR & AILSWORTH

Four miles west of Peterborough are the two villages of Castor and Ailsworth. There is no visible boundary between them except the village sign set up by the WI to commemorate their Golden Jubilee. Each village has its own character and identity although they have always shared the church and school. Ailsworth was originally a Saxon settlement and Castor named after 'Castra', a Roman camp. Ermine Street, the Roman road, crosses the Nene valley in a north westerly direction through the cornfields. The area around the road was the site of potteries where the distinctive Castor Ware was made. Many of the pots and jugs are decorated with hunting scenes on coloured glaze. This must have been a very prosperous place as a magnificent praetorium was built across the top of the hill where the church now stands. Excavations have unearthed baths, fine wallplaster, mosaics and many burials.

Ailsworth (the spelling of which has varied over the years), was a farming hamlet when in Saxon times Kyneburgha and her sister founded a nunnery in the ruins of the Roman house. Many artefacts including a comb, brooches, pins and domestic ware were unearthed among traces of humble wooden huts. The sisters' father was Penda, King of Mercia.

The 12th century church was dedicated to St Kyneburgha and is a fine example of Norman building. The magnificent tower has tiers of double arches with carved heads; the spire is a 14th century addition. Over the chancel door can be seen a Latin inscription which reads 'This church was dedicated on April 17th 1124'. Inside, on the north wall, can be seen a panel of three wall paintings depicting the martyrdom of St Catherine at the wheel, reputed to be one of only two known to exist.

Much of the 'old' villages still remains, stone-built houses and cottages, thatched or roofed with Collyweston slates. Some have been 'improved' beyond recognition, some demolished to make room for more modern developments, barns converted and most of the old stack yards infilled. Two paddocks, one in each village, have been preserved and are watched over with great care; these allow the opportunity to see animals and cherish the area's rural connections. Village Farm House, mostly 16th century, still has an Anglo-Saxon window and a dovecote mentioned in the Domesday Book; Castor House is Georgian; The Cedars, once the home of William Le Queux, (author of *Rasputin*) is 18th century; and the village hall was once the National School built by Lord Fitzwilliam in 1829.

Ailsworth village green sports a most magnificent horse chestnut tree planted on the site of the old village pond. It is a sheer delight when seen in full bloom. Just round the corner is the Methodist chapel, an oasis of village life, where Sunday services have been held since 1860; the schoolroom at the back serves many purposes but on Sundays reverts to its rightful role.

The villages rejoiced mightily in 1991 when the long-awaited A47 was officially opened – a project spanning 50 years was finally a reality. The former traffic chaos and pollution are now only memories, replaced by a wonderful sense of tranquillity, especially for those living alongside Peterborough Road.

🍁 CATWORTH

Catworth, or Cateworth as it was known in the 13th century, also includes the hamlet of Little Catworth. The village lies in the middle of the parish on the road from Kimbolton to Thrapston – part of the old coach road from London via St Neots to Oundle. The lovely village sign on the small green depicts the important farming industry of a community surrounded by three large farms.

The church is in the middle of the village and near to it are Glebe House (the old rectory), the former school which is now the village hall, and several 17th and 18th century houses.

At Brook End, about a quarter of a mile west of the village, is Brook House, added to and enlarged by Sir Felix Booth (about 1850), distiller and alderman of London. It incorporates part of a 16th century house and the hall has the original fireplace.

Long ago a bell was rung every Saturday at noon, maintaining a tradition that a stranger found men making hay on a Sunday, not knowing what day it was. He therefore left money to have a bell rung at noon on Saturday, that they might recognize the day.

Now Catworth is in the commuter belt, and the village has expanded in some ways and shrunk in others. In the not very distant past, there were three public houses, an off licence, three bakeries, two stores and a butcher's shop. Now it has one village store/post office, one public house (the Racehorse) within the village plus the Fox, a mile away on the A14 but still within the parish, and a petrol station/garage workshop. Many old houses remain and gradually modern houses and bungalows have crept in.

The church is 13th century and is beautiful inside and out, with fixed pews and an impressive brass chandelier holding candles.

🍁 CHERRY HINTON

The village sign, at the south end of Cherry Hinton High Street near the spring pool known as the Giant's Grave, shows a quartered shield with a steam plough, saffron flowers, washerwomen and a church, mounted on a cherry tree.

The village of Hinton, three miles south east of Cambridge and near the Gog Magog hills, has been in existence since Saxon times and there have been settlements in the area from the Iron Age. The earliest reference to Cherry Hinton is dated 1576, the name coming about because of the abundance of wild cherry trees in the area.

In the late 19th century and up until the 1930s, there was a manufacturing industry in the form of a steam plough works. The ploughs were hauled back and forth between two traction engines, the engines being too heavy for direct ploughing themselves.

Saffron plants were probably introduced into England by the Romans. The purple flowered plant with its bright yellow stamens was widely grown in the area until the early part of the 19th century and was used for cooking, dyeing and as a medicine for the 'ague'. The saffron grown here was considered to be the best in Britain.

The women of Cherry Hinton often took in college washing, with a regular donkey cart service taking bundles to and from Cambridge. Every open space was used as a drying ground but by 1888 the local laundry women had been replaced by the steam laundry.

The church on the sign is St Andrew's at the north end of the High Street. A church in Cherry Hinton is first mentioned in 1201 and the present building is Early English, the earlier Norman church having been rebuilt. Today it has a flourishing congregation and also provides a social centre for all ages from toddlers to senior citizens. The latest church to be built is the Church of Jesus Christ of Latter Day Saints which was opened in 1965. The Baptist church on Fishers Lane, built in 1883, has informal Sunday services led by a music group and has a family centre for community work.

Cherry Hinton village sign

Since 1935, Cherry Hinton has been absorbed into Cambridge administratively and its boundaries have become blurred, houses gradually covering open fields. There is a small industrial estate with light engineering and technology, and a new technology park is being built. Nearby Addenbrooke's Hospital is the biggest employer in East Anglia. The other major employer is Marshall's, just outside Cherry Hinton, where civil and military aircraft are refurbished in the huge hangar. Cherry Hinton has also become a commuter area, with people travelling daily as far afield as London.

The Cherry Hinton Village Centre, opened by Princess Diana in 1989, accommodates indoor sports and social activities. Pitches for outdoor sports are available on the nearby recreation ground, where the Cherry Hinton Festival is also held annually in September. The grounds of Cherry Hinton Hall (which looks Elizabethan but was built in the 19th century) are a pleasant leafy place. On Sunday afternoons in summer they ring to the sounds of brass bands or jazz combos. In July the Cambridge Folk Festival has been held here annually since 1964, its audiences coming from all over the country.

A bone of contention among residents is the traffic calming scheme in the High Street. If it were not there the street could become a race track, but is it too much? The village shops face tough competition from supermarkets in the area and unfortunately some have succumbed; but when you walk down the High Street, there is still always someone with whom to have a friendly chat.

🍁 CHESTERTON

Chesterton has been occupied since prehistoric times. The Roman farm site at Arbury gave the village its name. For many centuries it was an agricultural village but also had strong connections with the barge traffic on the river Cam, the barges coming from as far as Kings Lynn, and with the famous Stourbridge Fair for which it was the most important crossing of the river. Until quite recently, well in living memory, ferries took folk across the river from Chesterton to the Stourbridge Common side, making it quicker to reach the town of Cambridge. Its many inns, some now gone, must have provided accommodation for countless visitors who came to the fair not only from this country but from many parts of the world. The fair was very well known.

The river is the most prominent feature in Chesterton and is where the earliest settlers first built their homes. It is now a very large, spread out village, indeed it is hard to decide where Cambridge City ends and Chesterton begins!

Chesterton possesses many fine houses of differing architectural periods, one of which is reputed to be the oldest house in the area, at least by Chesterton inhabitants! It is well worth a visit even just to look at from the outside, and is situated not far from the parish church of St Andrew. It is called Chesterton Tower. Previous owners included the Abbot of Vercelli, in Northern Italy, whose representative lived there around 1279. Chesterton Hall is another fine old house dating from about 1650, a Jacobean building built of red bricks. It was much larger years ago and stood in extensive grounds. A Mayor of Cambridge once lived there but now what is left has been changed into flats by the City Council.

The parish church of St Andrew with its superb spire has been the centre of worship for more than 700 years. Inside, a very interesting Doom painting stretching over the chancel arch can be seen. Outside to the left of the porch is an unusual wall tablet commemorating the death of a young child who was the daughter of a freed African slave married to an Ely woman. There are also many interesting gravestones from which local history can be gathered, including one to Benjamin Jolley, known as Charon, a ferryman at the Pike and Eel for over 50 years. Many tales can be told about the ferrymen.

Other denominations are catered for in the village, too. It once had several chapels, one of which is now the Chesterton Workingmen's Club. There is a new chapel in Green End Road, where once a huge Iron Age hoard was found.

At the 'newer' end of Chesterton, off Milton Road, St George's church can be found. This was built in the 1930s to serve the ever growing population at this end of the village.

Chesterton has fine nursery, infants and primary schools, the last being St Andrew's Community School, built to replace the old Victorian school which was in the High Street opposite the shops, where now stand the houses in Primary Court.

CHEVELEY

Cheveley lies to the south east of Newmarket, off the B1063 road. In the late 1870s an anonymous poet left a record of his native village. He described the ruined castle in the park, near to which stood the mansion of the Duke of Rutland, 'who visits it every year'. The long street of the village, with its neat, small cottages, its village school, post office, shops, chapel and pub, was captured in verse. There was a blacksmith's shop too, 'and the name is Johnnie Deer'.

His words could easily be used as a guide for a stroll through Cheveley village today. Naturally change has come – gone are the mansion, the forge and the little shops while new houses have been built and tiles have replaced some thatched roofs. Agricultural land is now used by the many stud farms in the area for rearing racehorses. But the 12th century flint church with its unusual octagonal tower and attached barbican still stands proudly in the middle of the village and trees and green fields abound. It is to be hoped that as the village is not on a main thoroughfare it will long maintain its attractive air of calm and tranquillity.

🍁 CHIPPENHAM

Chippenham is a small East Anglian village, full of charm and character about five miles from Newmarket and, although surrounded by farmland, no longer an agricultural community. Around Chippenham Park Estate is a great wall more than three miles long. In the High Street you can see New Row with its colourwashed cottages. It is thought that there have been archaeological traces of early settlements within the parish boundaries.

William the Conqueror granted the Manor of Chippenham to one Geoffrey de Mandeville who died in 1086, the year of the Domesday Book, and was succeeded by his son William. The Chippenham Preceptory was also the infirmary for sick hospitallers; the Knights Hospitallers stayed in the village for three centuries.

The church is partly Norman in style, but evidence of the 13th century is seen, also Perpendicular work (the tower). More recently, the Tharp Chapel (the old Knights Hospitallers, chapel) was constructed by the Tharp family and dedicated by the Bishop of Ely in 1948. The church's patron saint is St Margaret of Antioch.

Thomas Beckett, who was owner of Chippenham Estate in the

Chippenham village sign

16th century, was knighted by Queen Elizabeth I during a royal visit here in 1578, died in 1582 and was buried in Chippenham where a monument to him is to be seen in the chancel of the church.

Lord Orford became the Lord of Chippenham and many years later Chippenham Estate became the property of John Tharp of Jamaica in February 1792. The Prince of Wales who became King Edward VII took part in partridge drives at Chippenham.

The school (now a private property) was built on the site of the Knights' Preceptory towards the end of the 17th century. Sadly, in July 1978, after so many years at the centre of village life, it was closed.

In February 1899, after a fire which started at a small farm in the centre of the village, much of that part of the village was destroyed, but cottages were rebuilt.

Two seats have been placed in the village to commemorate the Coronations of King George VI and Queen Elizabeth II. The bus shelter was opened by Lord Killanin in January 1949 and dedicated as a war memorial. The village sign which stands near the phone box was carved by the owner of the Deer Farm, following a competition held in the village for the final design. Although the population has increased, it has not been enough to keep the village shop, bakery and post office, all sadly closed down. Chippenham, however, remains a well sought-after village and Chippenham Fen nearby is now a National Nature Reserve.

🍁 CHRISTCHURCH

Christchurch is a small village situated in the heart of the fens, in what used to be known as the Isle of Ely. The surrounding fenland has some of the richest and most productive soil in the country, so farming is naturally its main industry, growing mainly corn, sugar beet and potatoes. Before the Second World War, almost everyone living in the village worked on the land, but since the introduction of modern machinery, very few workers are employed on the farms now.

In the early days the village was known as Brimstone Hill and belonged to the parish of Upwell, until the parish of Christchurch was created with the building of the church in 1865. For a long time Brimstone Hill remained, but the origin of the name is still a mystery. Some say it is from the Brimstone butterfly which inhabited the hill.

The Townley family financed the building of the church, as well as the village hall, formerly known as the Men's Institute. The village school built in 1932 is known as the Townley School, and the family coat of arms is on the school and the village sign. The workmen's hut used during building was sold when the church was completed and purchased by the village carpenter, Mr John Hiam, who moved it across the road and used it for his home. He named it 'The Ark' and it is still standing today.

Rev Sayers was rector of Christchurch between 1918 and 1928.

47

His daughter Dorothy L. Sayers was the author of many novels, in one of which, *The Nine Tailors*, Christchurch was mentioned.

There was a village blacksmith, Mr J. Rolfe, who was kept busy shoeing horses and repairing farm equipment. After the Second World War, his two sons Wolsey and Jack joined him, but the blacksmith's work began to change as tractors and modern machinery took over on the land. The workshop still remains in the village but is no longer used as a blacksmith's.

Water was piped to the village in 1912 and to locals it was known as Marham water because it came from a spring in a small Norfolk village called Marham. This, too, was a gift from the Townley family. A Methodist chapel was founded in 1872, but is now closed and has been made into a bungalow. After many years of service the post office has been closed and is being installed in the village shop. There were three public houses, but only one, the Dun Cow, now remains. However, a pavilion and playing field were provided in 1978 and there are many activities for members of the community to enjoy.

🍁 COATES

The very pretty village of Coates is on the A605 between March and Peterborough, on the northern edge of the fens, and is about ten feet above the surrounding areas which are five feet below sea level.

As late as the 1940s the main occupations were agriculture and the brickworks at Kings Dyke. There were four shops, four public houses, a blacksmith, miller, thatcher, cobbler and two carpenters who were also undertakers. Today there are three shops; two are general stores, one of which houses the post office, and the third is a butcher's. Two of the pubs have been closed and the other businesses have gone. Taking their place are two garages and a farm machinery sales and repair organisation.

Coates has one of the largest village greens in Cambridgeshire. The main road divides it in half. North Green is surrounded by very old large lime trees, but both greens have a variety of younger trees. In the past donkeys, horses and geese had the right to graze the greens. This finished when modern day traffic made it dangerous.

Old houses surround the greens, but most of the old thatched cottages have gone and new ones have been built in the spaces. Fortunately the new housing estates are behind the older properties.

The church is on the west side of North Green, with the church hall, the graveyard and the old rectory. The church was built in 1840. In 1987 a new rectory was built.

The chapel is a severe square building in the centre of North Green and was built in 1840 just before the church. Some villagers objected to the building, and during one night pulled down the work of the previous day, so chapel folk guarded the building until it was completed. It was enlarged in 1866.

The public house named the Carpenters Arms but known as the 'Top House' by locals is by the main road. Seats, swings and slides are on both greens. A very pretty lane called Cow Way leads from the bottom of North Green to the back of the village of Eastrea, about one mile away.

The Vine public house is on the South Green and close by is the old fire engine house, about the size of a modern garage. The engine was pumped by hand and also pulled by the men, and later by a pony called John Willy.

A very impressive village sign with scenes of long ago, horses, donkeys and geese on the green, with the church on one side and the chapel on the other, is one of the best to be seen in the area.

Approximately three quarters of a mile from the village is a small lane to Eldernell, where many centuries ago there was a Roman settlement. Now four farms and a ruined house that is said to be haunted, because a man and woman killed themselves in a bedroom, make up this pretty area that leads to washland. This often floods. Once it was all grassland but some of the land is now arable and very fertile too.

❧ COLNE

Colne is a very ancient settlement and probably got its name from the Latin word 'colonia' which means a colony. Two fairly large Romano-British sites have been excavated within the parish.

It has always been an agricultural village but with the coming of the railway, fruit became an important crop. This is no longer so as more farmers are turning their orchards over to cereals, sugar beet and other crops.

For some unknown reason the centre of the village has moved. The original church site, the moated site of one of the manor houses and the workhouse are a quarter of a mile from the present village centre. The time of this move is unknown. The tower of the original church fell down in 1896 and demolished most of the building. Permission was given for a new church to be built in the centre of the village. The £600 needed to build this new church was raised and the building was consecrated in 1900. Stones from the old church were incorporated in the new one. It is dedicated to St Helen. The small green in front of the church was originally the village pond and was filled in during the late 1960s.

Colne inhabitants were very prominent in the rise of Non-conformism in the area. They were particularly involved in the Baptist chapel at Bluntisham and eventually built their own small Baptist chapel in 1869. It is now a private bungalow.

The village was well served with public houses – there were eight in 1881 in a village of less than 400 inhabitants. Some had unusual names, such as the Spade and Bechet and the Red, White and Blue. The Green Man is the only one still a public house.

The village suffered from a serious fire in 1844, started by a disgruntled labourer from Bluntisham. Consequently, few very old houses remain.

A road in the village, close to the new church, is named after the family who owned one of the three Colne manors. Drury Lane is so

named after the Drury family whose London house was situated in a
road of the same name.

🍁 COMBERTON

Comberton is on the former main railway route from Cambridge to
Oxford. The local pronunciation is Cumberton. The Domesday Book
shows a population of around 200 in the 11th century.

William the Conqueror granted the manor of Comberton to
Erchanger, the baker. In return, he or his descendants baked a simnel
cake each day for the king until 1270 when the frequency was
reduced to one per week.

In 1863 the *Cambridge Chronicle* reported a case of witchcraft in
Comberton. On 28th February 1863 an inquest was held on Emma
Rust, aged 18, who had died from a succession of fits. The witnesses
believed that she had been bewitched by a Mrs Stonebridge but were
unable to say by what means this had been achieved.

Before 1914 the village was self sufficient with a blacksmith,
brewer, tailor, cobbler, farmers and farm labourers. Now few are
employed in agriculture and there is little local employment except
for small businesses, such as a plant nursery and a commercial
centre. The village has grown since the 1960s with new housing
estates and the population now exceeds 3,000.

The railway from Cambridge which passed near the village closed
in 1967. The line is now the home for numerous 'dishes' used for
research and observation in radio astronomy. This gives the area a
look of fantasy.

The National School was built at the crossroads in 1846 and is
now a nursery school. A turf maze, probably from the 17th century,
was in front of the main entrance. In 1908 it was recut in the
playground but was later covered over when the school was extended
in 1926. This village school was superseded by the Meridian School
(so named because the Greenwich meridian passes nearby) in 1968

and the Village College was opened in 1960.

The attractive village pond is at the centre of the village at the crossroads. The small village green around the pond was formerly marked by a stone cross but now has a painted wooden sign. One side depicts Comberton Mill which was blown down and the other side the distribution of the herrings from the Herringland Charity. This is the only local charity still in existence. The rent from eight acres purchased herrings to be given to the poor on Easter Day. Now the Parish Council distributes a token gift to needy villagers on Good Friday. The village sign was provided by funds raised for the Queen's Jubilee in 1977.

The parish church (St Mary's) celebrated its 700th anniversary with many varied events in 1987. It stands on high ground overlooking the village and surrounding countryside. Other interesting buildings are two dovecotes (converted to dwellings) and a number of picturesque thatched cottages.

🍁 COTON

'And Coton's full of nameless crimes', wrote the poet Rupert Brooke, but then he was prejudiced in favour of Grantchester, the better known village to which Coton was once joined.

It is situated some three miles west of Cambridge, a compact and convenient village of about 760 people with a fine new school, two popular pubs and flourishing village clubs and groups.

The name comes from the Anglo-Saxon word 'cotes', as in Domesday times it was only a collection of small cottages for workers on the several farms and has no hall or 'great house'. Those not employed on the farms worked in Cambridge and most still follow this pattern.

There are three large families, Sadlers, Cousins and Childerleys, whose names have dominated all village lists and teams for many years. Indeed when one Simon Childerley was landlord of the Plough

Inn, he was able to field his own family cricket team made up of himself, the seven sons out of his eleven children and three grandsons! There is a story of another celebrated match on the recreation ground when the visiting scorer, after finding that the bowler and the wicket keeper were both named Cousins, asked the name of one of the fielders and learnt it was also Cousins. 'What relation are they all? he asked innocently and all the spectators roared 'cousins'.

Back in 1880 there was a series of unsuccessful lawsuits when, after extensive coprolite digging had taken place in the village, the owners of the disturbed land claimed compensation. After several tries they ended by appealing unsuccessfully to the House of Lords and used up most of the village's charity money to help meet their costs.

There used to be a village pond, fed by the many springs. In 1953 it was filled in to tidy up the green outside the churchyard and promptly resurfaced in the rectory cellars which then had to be filled up also!

Nearby there is an interesting medieval dovecote, now in very poor condition, which has been restored in recent years.

The church has a Saxon font and a Norman window and a memorial to Andrew Downs, one of the scholars to make the Authorised translation of the Bible in the early 17th century. He retired from Cambridge to Coton, died here and is buried in the churchyard.

🍁 COTTENHAM

Cottenham is a thriving working village with a population of 4,870. It is now being expanded by 25%, or around 450 houses, an increase over the 1991 census return number of 1,739 dwellings.

The parish of Cottenham is a wedge-shaped piece of land of 7,231 acres, with its wide edge along the Old West River or Ouse and tapering to a flattened point 5½ miles to the south. Its 2 mile long village lies in the southern part of the parish on a ridge of Lower Green Sand which is 25 feet above sea level, whilst to the north are the fens, some being more than 15 feet below sea level.

There is evidence of Roman settlements in the fens, along the Car Dyke, or Old Tillage, where a considerable amount of pottery has been found. Earthworks of a Romano-British settlement can also be seen where Car Dyke crosses Cottenham Lode.

Thurcytel, a grandson of Alfred the Great, gave the manor of Crowland in Cottenham in AD 971 to Crowland Abbey in Lincolnshire in return for kindness shown to him there. Tradition says that Cottenham played a part in the founding of the University of Cambridge. After an abbey fire in 1109, four learned monks from Crowland came to reside on their estate there, hired a barn in Cambridge and attracted a large crowd to their lectures. The Coteham of Domesday had a population of 350 and was comprised of three manors which became six by the time of the Hundred Rolls in 1278. Some Cottenham streets are named after the manors.

Manorial records of Crowland documented, in 1290, the name of Willelmus Pepiz who cultivated a ten acre plot of servile land for which he performed annually 51 'works' on his lord's demesne and rendered in money 4s 6½ d. The family of Pepys rose rapidly in status after the Black Death, becoming bailiffs, then yeoman farmers, until the time of John Pepys. John, who was the great grandfather of Samuel, the diarist, married a weathly heiress. The present Earl of Cottenham is a direct descendant. Katherine Pepys, the last of that name in Cottenham, endowed the Pepys school and left a charity which still exists today.

Calvin Coolidge, President of the USA (1923–29), was descended from a Cottenham Coolidge family. John Coolidge, born in 1604, crossed the Atlantic in 1630 to become one of the early New England settlers.

John Tenison, a curate of Cottenham church, was the father of Archbishop of Canterbury Thomas Tenison, and a former rector,

William Warham, also became Archbishop of Canterbury.

All Saints' church, so called in 1403, was rebuilt in Perpendicular style in the 15th century. Its tower, demolished in a storm in 1617, was rebuilt with bulbous pinnacles which give a striking appearance when viewed from afar. Cottenham's Dissenters Cemetery was opened in 1845. Over 4,000 people have been buried there to date.

Two thirds of Cottenham was destroyed by fire in 1676 and many of the older houses seen today date back to rebuilding at that time. Later fires in 1847 and 1855 destroyed more houses, which were rebuilt in a uniform style of yellow Cottenham brick from clay dug from the pits of Ivatt Street.

Sheep rearing was important in the 16th century when Sir Francis Hinde of Madingley, who had bought the manors of Crowland and Lisles, began to enclose the drier parts of the commons for his use. A detailed Agreement in 1596, ratified in Chancery, settled disputes and established the basis on which the commons were managed until 1842. Twelve gentlemen and clergy and 109 others signed the Agreement. Under it 167 householders had a right of common allowing them to keep up to ten cows or horses and ten sheep. A thyme-like herbage grew on the fens which flavoured the cows' milk. The parish specialised in making a cheese which was famous throughout England. Two varieties were made, one a hard Stilton-like cheese and the other the single Cottenham. Cheese making rapidly declined after the 1842 enclosure when the commons were ploughed up, giving way to arable land.

Commercial market gardening began. Later, commercial fruit growing was introduced. The area used rose from 200 acres in 1885 to 1,500 in the 1930s, covering much of the ridge. Asparagus, apples, plums, gooseberries, pyrethrums and strawberries were the most important crops. Up to 500 acres of strawberries were grown after the Second World War but declined to five acres in 1990. Orchards were grubbed up after 1950 when younger people found it more profitable to work in Cambridge or with the increasing number of small firms around the village.

The October Feast, an old custom, is still celebrated every year on the first Sunday after 11th October. A parade is organised and most of the local associations enter a decorated float.

🍁 COVENEY & WARDY HILL

Coveney and Wardy Hill are two small villages set on 'islands' above the fen, a mile apart, about four miles west of Ely. They are run as one parish, but are two completely separate villages in many ways. Coveney derives its name from 'island in the bay', and not from anything to do with witches, as many people would like to think. Wardy Hill comes from 'warden's hill' or look-out.

The main industry in the villages is agriculture. There are many farms of various sizes and these are mainly arable – the crops grown are potatoes, sugar beet, corn and onions. Up until the 1950s most people in the villages worked on the farms, both men and women. The women usually did jobs like weeding, 'chopping out' sugar beet and helping with the potato harvest. As the farms have become more mechanised, not so many people work on the land.

Coveney is not mentioned in the Domesday Book, but was first mentioned in 1060 when the manor was given to Aethelswyth for life in return for her gift to Ely Priory of her life interest in Stetchworth. She settled in Coveney with her maidens to work at embroidery and weaving. Wardy Hill is first mentioned in a document in 1251 – but there must have been a settlement here long before, as Bronze Age shields and swords have been found in the area.

Coveney church of St Peter ad Vincula dates back to the 13th century with building going on during the 14th and 15th centuries. It was thatched until 1896 when the tiled porch was added. Coveney has a Methodist chapel and it also had a Baptist chapel which was in use from 1833 to 1906. It can still be seen at the end of Mansion Farm house, and gravestones are still in the front garden. Mansion Farm is the oldest house in the village. It is thought to have been built at the same time as the church, and some of the fireplaces are built of the same Barnack stone. The roof is thatched, with a plaster front and many fine beams. The front door is very old and is still barred not locked. It is the only thatched house left in the village.

Another interesting building is the village pound found next to the pond. The date on the pound is 1840, but it is thought to be earlier. It was used to impound cattle that had wandered away from the common grazing areas.

Next to the pound is the village lock-up; this was actually used for housing the village bier which carried the coffins to church. The village pond and grass area around was cleared by the Parish Council in 1960. Here stands the village sign, presented to the village by the WI in 1977 to commemorate the Queen's Silver Jubilee; it is made of wood and was carved by Mr Carter of Swaffham in Norfolk. It is very colourful and shows Aethelswyth doing her embroidery, and a man from Wardy Hill looking out for cattle raiders coming across the fen. Wardy Hill has its own village green, a most attractive feature for the village.

🍁 CROXTON

In August 1887, 800 men and women sat down to a roast beef and plum pudding dinner at Croxton Park by invitation of Mr Newton, the owner of the house and most of the surrounding land. Children had tea afterwards and participated in sports, and there was dancing and fireworks until 10 pm, when *God Save the Queen* was sung. If you visited Croxton today you might wonder where all these people came from. Some would have been from Eltisley as the villages are very close and the owners of Croxton Park owned land in Eltisley and employed workers from there too, but it is apparent that Croxton is a village which until recently had a declining population.

Croxton village today mainly comprises two parallel roads running off the A428, plus a few houses along this busy main road, four miles east of St Neots and 13 miles west of Cambridge. One road, with the Spread Eagle public house on the corner (which pulled its last pint for Greene King on Sunday 8th November 1998 after serving locals and through traffic on the main road for over a century) leads to Abbotsley; it has the lands of Croxton Park on one side and 20 houses on the other. The last two houses lie at the bottom of a hill and every spring hundreds of frogs cross the road here to find water to lay their spawn and then cross back again, and then a few weeks later hundreds of young frogs attempt the crossing – drivers please take note and take care!

The other village road is the older inhabited part and leads to the gates of the Park and also to the church of St James. The church was built in 1280 but there had been an earlier church on the same site. The present church has retained its 13th century font and pre-Reformation pews, though they are much weathered, possibly due to damage done to the building by Cromwell's army. It is said that the teeth marks of their horses can be seen in the woodwork! Croxton has certainly changed – the original village was on a road between the church and where the big house stands, but none of this village now exists at all. The last of the original village houses were demolished by the owner of the Park in 1780 and the site converted into a lake, but the village had been moving to is present position for many years before that. The present Croxton Park was built in 1760 by Edward Leeds but the Leeds family had lived there in an earlier house on the same site since 1571. The Leeds family owned the house, farmlands and virtually the whole parish until 1825. Since then the land has been sold and divided, and several old 'estate' houses have disappeared. Among those left are a pretty cottage to one side of the Park gate and a late medieval timber-framed house on the other side, facing a small green.

There used to be a school on the main road, built in 1869 by George Newton, who also paid the school mistress's wages of £50 a year. By 1896 it was attended by 117 children from Croxton and Eltisley, but now the few children of primary school age living in the village attend the Newton County Primary School in Eltisley.

Croxton shares a rector with Eltisley, Graveley, Yelling, Toseland and Papworth St Agnes.

🍁 DODDINGTON

'There are immense marshes, now a black pool of water, now a foul running stream, and also many islands . . .' wrote an 8th century monk of the area. Doddington is situated on one of those islands. The original parish of Doddington covered 37,801 acres, the largest in Cambridgeshire. In the Middle Ages, Doddington was one of the most important places in the Isle of Ely, but very few memorials of the past still exist. The only important pieces of architecture are the village cross – 14th century with a modern head, the remains of an early 19th century tower windmill, a round house, the clock tower and the church.

The church of St Mary the Virgin has a long history with the chancel and part of the north aisle dating back to the 13th century. The tower contains eight bells with dates ranging from 1736 to 1936. They are often to be heard ringing out across the fens as campanologists visit from all over the country. A famous rector of Doddington was Christopher Tye, the organist at St George's Chapel, Windsor. In 1560 he wrote the music for the Christmas carol *While shepherds watched their flocks by night*.

The village school bears the name of Lionel Walden who in his will dated 1719, directed that his property should be sold and the interest on the proceeds be allowed to accumulate until it reached £500. This sum was then to be used to build a school at Doddington.

Right in the centre of the village stands the clock tower, built to commemorate Queen Victoria's Diamond Jubilee. Originally it stood in the middle of the road at the junction of Benwick Road and High Street. Because of the increase in traffic, it was taken down brick by brick and rebuilt at the side of the road. In 1897 the clock had four faces, now there are only three.

Another interesting feature of Doddington is the 'Round House'. It was built in the days of mud and wattle, but was partly demolished in 1949. A new section was built on the back. It is the original round house, complete with thatched roof, that is seen from the road. Although it has all the conveniences of a modern bungalow, it retains its old world charm and is unique to the district.

As in most villages, farming is the main industry. Cereals, potatoes and sugar beet do particularly well in the rich fen soil. Some years ago a small brickyard provided work but all that remains now is Brickmakers Arms Lane and the brickyard pit. The pit is said to have been as deep as the church is high.

The North Witchford Union Workhouse was opened in 1838, but in 1941 it was officially upgraded as a hospital under the wartime Emergency Medical Scheme. It served as a small General Hospital until 1988. The Workhouse Buildings are no longer used and there is now a Community Hospital housed in modern buildings on the same site.

The two public houses, the Three Tuns and the George, are now, as always, the hub of village life and are home to numerous darts and dominoes teams. Doddington also has a new pavilion and sports field where football, cricket, tennis and bowls are played.

🍁 DOWNHAM-IN-THE-ISLE

The first record of this village was when the manor of Dounham was given to the monks of Ely in the year AD 970.

The manor grew in importance during the Middle Ages when the 'Hall' or 'Palace' became the favourite residence of the Bishops of Ely. It was at the end of the 15th century that the palace was reconstructed by the great Bishop Alcock. He was a discriminating builder and as Master of the Rolls one of the most important judges in the country. A chapel in Ely Cathedral is dedicated to him.

Perhaps the two best known bishops who stayed at Downham were Lancelot Andrewes and Matthew Wren. Bishop Andrewes was a great authority on languages and was responsible for translating the Authorised Version of the Bible from Genesis to the Second Book of Kings. Bishop Matthew Wren was a staunch Royalist and High Churchman. He was an uncle to the famous Christopher.

The ending of the bishops' regime in Downham came with the arrival of the Dutch engineer Vermuyden and the fen drainage which revealed the rich black soil as we know it today.

There were few houses in early times but a lot of cattle and bulls. These were tended by a few men on stilts and they could cover the ground very quickly on these.

Later as the village grew there were more cottages, and many public houses, where quite a lot of drunkenness went on. From the 1890s to the Second World War years an annual feast was held on the first Sunday in June, and for the following three days. On Feast Sunday, as it was called, caravans would roll into the village pulled by cart-horses. This was a most exciting time for children. On Feast Sunday, most homes had new potatoes (home grown of course), perhaps peas too and always gooseberry pie. Dad was a poor gardener indeed if he could not supply these!

Every January, on Plough Sunday, a plough is carried into the parish church of St Leonard for a service of blessing and prayers for the sowing and reaping of the crops in the coming year, also for the animals and all who work on the land.

Downham is still an agricultural village. Once much fruit was grown here in orchards and every cottage garden, but the orchards have now gone. Strawberries and raspberries are however very plentiful.

Downham has a few tales of ghosts, the most famous a monk who is supposed to appear in a certain bedroom of the old rectory and in the church grounds. One rector of not so many years ago claims a bed was taken down in bits during the night and bells rang, but no one was seen!

🍁 DUXFORD

Duxford parish is roughly triangular, about 3 miles long and 1½ miles at its widest point. Its north east corner at Whittlesford Bridge holds Duxford's Chapel, an Ancient Monument, about 12th century, also the Red Lion public house, once a hospital for the Knights Templars. At this point it is about 80 feet above sea level. It rises to about 300 feet on Pepperton Hill, from where you can overlook the M11 motorway and the 'Ciba Geigy' (now Novartis) factory.

The present village is made up of two separate parishes – Duxford St Peter and Duxford St John, which accounts for the two churches, both 12th century, and the network of footpaths which used to run through the centre. St John's church fell into disuse about 1877 and is now in the care of the Redundant Churches Council. The bells from St John's were transferred to St Peter's.

The majority of labour was centred on the farming community until the millers gradually changed from corn to grinding bones for fertilizer. In about 1853 one mill changed again, this time to coprolite, also for fertilizer, and the Cambridge Fertilizer Company was formed. This was taken over by Fisons Brothers and later still by Mr Shirling Rooke; this was the only attempt at manufacture until Mr N. De Bruyne started Aero Research in 1934, now 'Ciba Geigy' (Novartis). In the First and Second World Wars, Duxford was synonymous with its airfield and the population got steadily larger (now about 1,750). The airfield is now occupied by the Imperial War Museum.

Duxford has had a village school since the mid 18th century. (The *Cambridge Chronicle* carried an advertisement for a School Master in about 1770.) Lessons were held in a vestry of St John's church, but in 1847 the National School was built in St Johns Street for 30 pupils. Later a headmaster and a school mistress were employed as the pupil numbers increased, the headmaster living rent free in the adjoining house with an annual salary of £50, the school mistress earning

£25. In 1960 another new school was built to take pupils from Duxford, Hinxton, Ickleton and Duxford Airfield.

There are about 20 listed buildings in Duxford, probably the oldest of these being the Manor House in Green Street (14th century) and College Farm House next to St John's church (15th century), both of which show timber framing of the original building. Both have been extensively altered, but by far the most noteworthy renovation is Duxford Mill, mentioned in the Domesday Book, but later burnt down and rebuilt in about the 15th century with later additions in the 16th century. This must be classed as a success story, as it was quite dilapidated and overgrown when Mr R. Lea took it in hand and recreated magnificent lawns, the mill pool and superb rose gardens. It has had some notable visitors in its past. It is said that the inspiration for Charles Kingsley's book *The Water Babies* was gained here on one of his many visits. It is now open regularly to the public.

🍁 EARITH

This is a small, quiet village of around 3,000 inhabitants. It lies twelve miles north of Cambridge, with the once county town of Huntingdon some twelve miles to the west.

Earith in some respects is the gateway to the fens and from its western elevated boundary, which incidentally runs right through the middle of the 14th century St Mary's church shared by the villages of Earith and Bluntisham, can be seen fine views of the fens to the Isle of Ely. Just below the church lies Bury and Little Fens, a scene of many memorable skating races and the birthplace of 'Bandy' or ice hockey. Even today, weather permitting, the Fen Speed Skating Championships are still held on this area of the fen, a far cry from the modern indoor speed skating as seen at the Olympics but equally, if not more so, as exciting.

The village, which is nestled between the watery junction of the Great Ouse river and the man-made Bedford Levels, was once a highly developed inland port, hence the translation of the word Earith which means 'muddy harbour', and merchandise, usually timber, was brought inland from the Wash. It was this timber trade which led to the great East Anglian firm of Messrs Jewson and Sons starting their business over 100 years ago.

The village during the 18th and early 19th centuries was one of great prosperity and the Earith Fairs were famous for miles around. Many a passing pedlar, cattle dealer or bargee would stop in the village to refresh himself at one of the numerous inns or public houses, most of which have disappeared today.

The village, although small, has a history and charm all of its own. This part of the country being the birthplace of Oliver Cromwell, it has retained a great deal of the history of that period. Evidence of this can be seen by proceeding through the main street of the village to the river bridge, where on the far side looking towards Ely can be seen a large earthworks called 'The Bulwark'. This structure was built as a defensive fort to house cannon and the like to defend the waterways from the Royalists. Although the village is no longer a centre of trade and business, the population has not declined, in fact it has increased.

The modern village of Earith has tried to retain that all-important balance of history and progress. It has a modern school, catering for both infant and primary education, a post office and general store, a local baker, and a ladies' hairdresser. There are also two marinas. Efforts have been made to ensure that those houses that have been built or renovated in the main street through the village retain an appearance that is in keeping with their predecessors.

🍁 ELM

This once peaceful village still centres on its fine church of All Saints, much as it did 600 years ago. The church records go back that far, when there was both a rector and a vicar looking after the living. The

Bishop settled a dispute in 1395 when 'unseemly bloodshed' had occurred in the chancel over tithes, and finally the rector received 'all the tithes of sheaves of Wheat, Barley, Oats, Rye, Beans, Peas, Straw and Flax' while the vicar got 'all the Wool, Lambs, Calves, Porkers, Milk, Cheese, Bee's Honey and Wax'.

There was great parochial unrest when proposals were made to lay a tramline through the village in 1881, even a petition sent to Parliament. The tramway was laid from Wisbech to Upwell alongside the canal. Alas neither have survived, the tramway was a victim of Dr Beeching and the canal was filled in when the Anglian Water Authority rerouted the drainage in the fens. Many of the villagers remember the tramway and the canal, which was well used in the past, particularly on Saturday nights when revellers came home from Wisbech by barge, singing all the way!

The schools have also changed. A hundred years ago only boys went to Elm and Emneth Church School and paid 2d a week, and the girls went to a private school situated where the present post office is today by Elm Bridge.

Many of today's residents were born here, married and stayed to have their families. Nobody wants to leave Elm and many want to come! There are of course many more houses now, a change from the 19th century when the scattered cottages all had their own small-holding or at least a large cottage garden. It is still an agricultural area with fruit, vegetables, flowers and grains being harvested throughout the year, but most of the newcomers go further afield to work.

Social life centres round the church, church house, four public houses and the two village shops. In the 1920s there were five bakers in the village and the smell of new bread was wonderful!

There have been changes, but in some ways the pattern of life does not change at all and in the old names such as Rose Lane, Halfpenny Lane, Begdale and Gosmore you can hear the ripple of the stream that once flowed through the village.

🍁 ELSWORTH

Elsworth (Elli's enclosure) lies on the western plateau, south of the Cambridgeshire Fens. As its name implies, it is an Anglo-Saxon settlement. It developed along the banks of the brook which flows through the village from south to north into the Ouse at Swavesey. Elsworth gives its name to an outcrop of Jurassic limestone, 160 million years old, found in and to the north of the village. The rock contains molluscs and ammonites which are unique to the locality, and it outcrops in the bed of the brook. In this area the vertebrae of an ichthyosaurus and the leg-bone of a dinosaur have been unearthed.

A wood at Elsworth was recorded in 1279 and still flourishes today. It contains one of the best examples of field maple in Cambridgeshire, together with hazel and oak. All down the years Elsworth has been an agricultural village. In medieval times the Abbot of Ramsey was lord of the manor; everyone worked on the land and the chief crops grown were wheat, barley, peas and oats. Farming still dominates the scene, but fewer than a dozen living in the parish are farm workers and the crops are reduced to wheat and rape. There are old men and women, born and bred in the village with their parents and grandparents before them, who hark back to the days of harvest homes and working horses. They tell of potato picking and threshing, of pea pulling and hedge laying and of other back-breaking jobs.

The last of the wheelwrights, John Throssell, died in 1988 at the age of 99. His business developed into carpentry and building. There is a garage – the modern equivalent of the smithy – a post office and two hairdressers.

Community life in the village is centred on the church, the primary school and the sports field. The church is 14th century and is notable for being almost entirely of one period. It is built of local field stone and local limestone rubble, and today the upkeep of its fabric drains the energies and resources of the rector and his parishioners. The sports field, or Grass Close by its old name, is the

Elsworth village

park of the manor house. The Manor was built in 1660 by Samuel Desborough for his second wife, Sarah. It is now divided into four dwellings. Samuel was the brother of Cromwell's general, John Desborough, who married Cromwell's sister.

Elsworth is a thriving rural community, proud of its quiet heritage symbolised in the village sign. This depicts an ammonite, a shield bearing the arms of the Abbot of Ramsey, the Domesday Book, the church tower, sprays of wheat and a cartwheel. It was erected as a tribute to the aforesaid John Throssell MBE, the parish clerk for 54 years, a fine craftsman and a true countryman.

❧ ELTISLEY

Eltisley is a small village five miles east of St Neots and twelve miles west of Cambridge, bypassed by the A428. It is mentioned in the Domesday Book as Hecteslei, which means an Anglo-Saxon settlement in a wooded area. There is still part of this ancient wood existing but is now in private hands. The population varied from 27 in 1086 to a maximum of 504 in 1871 and now stands at around 350.

The centre of the village is a beautifully kept triangular green surrounded by attractive houses, with three horse chestnut trees, one in each corner. These were planted in 1887 to commemorate Queen Victoria's Golden Jubilee and are known as Faith, Hope and Charity. The green was common land and each April the parish council let it by auction for pasture. As recently as 1947 cows were walked along to the side greens to graze and goats were tethered there. In summer now the main recreation on the green is cricket, players and spectators taking tea afterwards in the thatched cricket pavilion presented to Eltisley Cricket Club by James Cade in 1935 in memory of his father Joseph Cade, who was born in the village.

Leading eastwards away from the green along Caxton End is a line of lime trees known as the Row of Honour. These were planted during the First World War to commemorate each man from Eltisley who died. In January 1919 three trees were placed to form the Cross of Sorrow and in March 1919 the Peace Tree (an evergreen) was planted at the head of the line 'with the help of four brave survivors'.

A further reminder of the price paid by Eltisley in the First World War is the lychgate at the church; engraved on either side are the names of those who fell. An avenue of pollarded limes leads to the church of St Pandionia and John the Baptist, built around 1200 near the site of a monastery which was among the oldest in England. Pandionia was the daughter of a Scottish king who fled to a kinswoman (the prioress of Eltisley nunnery) to avoid marrying the man chosen for her by her father. Pandionia died there and was buried beside a well, which also carried her name. The well, in the churchyard, was a centre for pilgrimage until 1570, when it was destroyed by the rector, Robert Palmer, to 'prevent its use for superstitious purposes'. Her body, however, had been moved into the church in 1344.

Another legend which has grown up around the church concerns the famine in July 1234, when starving peasants raided local farmers' fields for food. The farmers were incensed and marched to the church the following Sunday and all, except one, asked the rector to excommunicate the offenders. He had hardly started to pronounce the sentence when a great storm blew up, destroying crops, livestock and buildings and devastating the whole area – with the exception of the lands and possessions of the one farmer who had not objected. These happenings are shown on the village sign.

Next door to the church is a large house built in 1612 by James Desborough, whose son John married Oliver Cromwell's sister Jane in Eltisley church in 1636. On the opposite side of the green is the oldest house in the village built late 15th century, early 16th, and called the Old Post Office. The Leeds Arms, on the corner of the green, is the only remaining pub out of five formerly in the village. It was built in 1814 and also acted as a place where inquests were held in the late

Eltisley village green

1800s. The Cambridgeshire Hunt meets outside on Boxing Day, when the village is packed with people and cars.

A century ago, Eltisley boasted two shopkeepers, a tobacconist, bricklayer, shoemaker, butcher and grocer, poultry dealer, poulterer, two wheelwrights, blacksmith, carpenter, two pubs, a boot and shoemaker, thatcher, coal dealer and eleven farmers. In 1998, sadly, there are no shops and no post office, but Eltisley remains a pleasant and friendly village to live in, with several thriving groups catering for different ages and interests. The Newton County Primary School in Caxton End, is attended by approximately 100 pupils from 4 to 11 years and takes in children from Yelling, Graveley, Toseland, Croxton and Papworth St Agnes, as well as Eltisley.

🍁 ELTON

Elton is situated on the borders of Cambridgeshire and Northamptonshire. Five miles to the east is the edge of the fens and to the west extends the area which was Rockingham Forest in medieval times. The river Nene flows through the valley at the lower end of the village and marks the boundary between the two counties.

Elton is a large parish extending to nearly 4,000 acres. Fifty years ago Elton was a village very different from today, with five working farms and cows walking in all the streets to the farms to be milked. Today Elton is a dormitory village for Peterborough with new housing estates and old cottages and barns being refurbished, but still retaining its beauty with the village greens and lovely old chestnut trees.

Elton has been inhabited since prehistoric days. Early farmers settled in the parish around 6,000 years ago and from then on agriculture has been most important to the village. There are five Roman sites in Elton and a major Roman road linking two important Roman towns which can still be traced through the eastern part of the parish. It was not until the Saxon period that Elton got a name similar to that which it bears today. The Saxon settlers laid out the parish boundary, built the church and set up two manors, and many of their fields carried on right up to the time when the parish was enclosed in the 1790s. There are two Saxon gravestones at the north side of the church.

One of the most notable features of Elton is the park area, lying between the church and Elton Hall, which remains largely unaltered since the medieval period. It was possibly first created for deer hunting by the lord of the manor and was then converted for extensive sheep rearing. Later it was landscaped for the Earls of Carysfort who lived at the hall. Elton Hall was one of the Saxon manors – it was never a castle, but was defended. For the last 400 years it has been the home of the Proby family.

People who visit the hall can stroll along Overend and call in at the church. The tower of the church was probably built by the same man who built the Sapcot Tower at Elton Hall round about 1500. In addition to the notable tower, the monuments of the Proby family and the William Morris stained glass windows, the church is very pleasant with commanding views to the west over the Nene valley.

One can walk down Middle Street, admire the stone and thatch cottages and on to the other end of the village, to Stocks Green where previously there was a set of stocks. A watermill that was mentioned in the Domesday Book can be seen here. Nearby is the Crown Inn, set back from the green and sheltering under the shade of the chestnut tree.

🍁 EYNESBURY

Eynesbury is divided from St Neots by the Hen Brook on the north side whilst the river Ouse separates it from Eaton Socon on the west side. The parish also contains three hamlets, Weald, Caldecot and Eynesbury Hardwick.

There is evidence of Eynesbury's early occupation in the Stone and Bronze Ages and the Iron Age. In the Roman and Saxon periods evidence shows the expansion of the settlement in both the Hen Brook and river areas.

As time passed the village developed into a pleasant one and as agriculture became the main form of livelihood several large farmhouses and farmyards were built. The cottages occupied by the farm workers were mainly terraced, but there were also some attractive thatched and timber framed houses, a few of these being lived in today.

In the oldest part of Eynesbury stands the church of St Mary, the register of which dates back to 1539. A Methodist chapel was built in 1855 and a new chapel built near the site of the original one in 1928.

In St Mary's Street in the past, sufficient small shops supplied the needs of the Eynesbury inhabitants and, as in neighbouring St Neots, there were many public houses. Several of these licensed premises survive today, serving the public with both food and drink, but the old shops have become updated or pulled down, and more traders have now opened premises to serve in various ways the ever growing population.

There still remain the two public open spaces which have been there for centuries. Eynesbury Green, on which May Day was annually celebrated, now contains several red chestnut and lime trees which are a delight in the spring and early summer. Eynesbury Coneygear, so named because it was a rabbit warren in the past, is a large open space near the river Ouse. Eynesbury Feast Day, the Sunday nearest to the 8th September, used to be celebrated here.

The only really notable people Eynesbury can boast of are James Toller, the Eynesbury Giant, and the St Neots Quads. James Toller was born in Rectory Lane in 1798 and his height at the age of 18 was 8' 1½". In 1815 he was exhibited in London and there presented to foreign Royalty. He died in 1818, being then 8' 6" tall. In more recent times Eynesbury was put on the map because of the birth in November 1935 of the St Neots Quads, as they were always referred to. The four babies were born to Mrs Doris Miles, of Ferrera Avenue, with only the local doctor and midwife in attendance.

In the early 1960s St Neots, with Eynesbury, became a London Overspill area. There are now various factories and places of employment here, far removed from the agricultural industry which many older residents remember. In addition to the council housing estates, large private estates have been built.

🍁 FEN DITTON

Fen Ditton is a small village situated on the north eastern outskirts of Cambridge. At the 1991 census the population stood at 700. Fen Ditton has a fine 14th century church, a school, a shop with a post office and four public houses – it once had five! The houses include several large ones of 17th century vintage, a few even older, a sprinkling of thatched cottages and a row of attractive almshouses with pretty gardens. Most homes, of course, date from the 19th century up to the present day, the most recent ones being positioned according to the principle of 'in-filling'.

The jewel in Fen Ditton's crown is the river Cam that flows past it, creating a peaceful scene as it winds its way between banks lined with willow trees. Rowing eights are a familiar sight as they go up and down this stretch of river practising for the May Bumps and other races. In the past, however, the river was made use of for a far more serious purpose than pleasure. It was the main means of transport, with barges bringing coal and other goods up from the Wash via the Ouse to the Cam. This accounts for the oldest part of the village being adjacent to the river and it is believed that an ancient barn now belonging to the Hall was formerly a warehouse.

From 1885 another means of transport was the railway. Fen Ditton had a halt on the Cambridge-Mildenhall line until the line was closed by Beeching in the sixties.

Before the motor car became a common possession, farm work

St Mary the Virgin, Fen Ditton

was the main occupation of the male population, while osier cutting and coprolite digging provided alternative employment on a smaller scale. Then gradually men began drifting away from the land to work for the nearby Marshall's Airport or Pye Radio Communications. Once they had cars there was no limit to their place of employment. The farms themselves were becoming mechanised and did not need so many workers. Eventually they were affected by the encroachment of the city and farmers gave up altogether, selling some of their land for building. Out of the three major ones that existed twenty years ago there is now only one working farm left.

Although it is easy to get to Cambridge for entertainment the village provides quite a lot towards its inhabitants' social life. There are badminton and gardening clubs, a Women's Institute and a good recreation ground which some years ago was levelled out on common land known as Campo. A pavilion on it was built by voluntary labour.

Fen Ditton is indeed a very pleasant place to live in, yet not without its problems. The volume of traffic passing through it via Horningsea Road to gain access to the busy A14 cuts the village in two at peak times. Protests have been made and alternative approaches are being considered. Fen Ditton is also in danger of losing its independence by being one of the so-called 'necklace' villages much coveted by Cambridge City Council who would like to absorb it into the city. Any threats of this kind are always fiercely resisted by most villagers who would prefer it to remain a county village in its own right and are consequently in favour of retention of the Green Belt.

It is hoped that this beautiful village will retain its individuality and peaceful atmosphere for many years to come.

🍁 FEN DRAYTON

The spire of St Mary's church can be seen from the very busy A14 trunk road, one mile away. A 'fen-edge' village, nine miles from Cambridge and seven from Huntingdon, Fen Drayton is still relatively small and tranquil.

Entering the village from the Huntingdon direction brings you past the horticultural area, where lettuce, tomatoes, celery and flowers such as chrysanthemums are still grown. Originally formed as the 'Land Settlement Association' in the 1930s to provide employment for miners and others from the depressed areas of the north and Wales, the holdings have now been sold and some are no longer commercial enterprises. However, one of the largest and most modern glasshouse complexes in the region, covering some 10 acres, is currently under construction.

The oldest part of the village, where evidence of occupation during Roman times has been excavated, is a conservation area and still retains a number of fine old buildings.

St Mary's church is built on the highest ground at 23 feet above sea level. Evidence of a Saxon building can still be seen in its fabric. Mentioned in Pevsner's *Buildings of England*, interesting features such as a 'leper window' are noted.

Fronting the High Street are several houses of note: Home Farm, a fine 16th/17th century half-timbered yeoman's farmhouse; Old Manor Farm, a 16th/17th century red-brick-faced farmhouse with two 'eleven step' gable ends and other Dutch features, reminding us that Dutch drainage engineers operated in this region during the 17th/18th century, draining the wet fen for agricultural land; the Merchant's House, a fine red brick house of around 1730 with Dutch influence gable ends and limestone cappings, fronting an earlier timber-framed building; the Three Tuns public house, a late 15th/ early 16th century timber-framed building, with jettied crosswing with very fine moulded beams and carved central boss, thought originally to have been the village trade or guild hall. Also of interest is the 19th century village lock-up, with its two windowless cells attractively situated by the village stream (or brook).

Fen Drayton Brook runs through the village, draining water from the higher land to the south, down to the great Ouse river one mile to the north. Many times over the years Fen Drayton, like many local villages, has suffered flooding; in more recent times, most notably in 1947, but also as recently as 1998.

A village of some 750 people, Fen Drayton has recently seen its shop close, although it retains the post office, village garage and a thriving primary school.

Farming is still an important part of the rural scene here, although most villagers commute to work in Cambridge or Huntingdon or as far afield as London.

🍁 FENSTANTON

Fenstanton with its population of approximately 2,600 stands on the A14, nine miles from Cambridge and five miles from Huntingdon.

The nearest neighbouring town is St Ives, the water meadows of which join those of Fenstanton. The village is well supplied with shops and in the early morning the smell of freshly baked bread wafts temptingly on the air. The main source of employment in the village is the Unigate Dairies. The farms, having become so mechanised, now only employ very few people.

The parish church dedicated to St Peter and St Paul, built of rubble dressed with stone, is recorded in The Domesday Book of 1086. During the 13th and 14th centuries the church was enlarged considerably and a most beautiful chancel was built. On one of the chancel buttresses is an old mass dial and near to it within the churchyard is the base of a stone cross, the date of which is unknown. Was it perhaps the old preaching cross, used before the first stone church was built?

In the centre of the older part of the village, at the bottom of the High Street, stands the Clock Tower, built in the second part of the 1600s. This building has been put to various uses. At one time market taxes were collected there, at another period it was used as the village lock-up. The stocks are still kept within its walls, though thankfully not used in this day and age.

Fenstanton, like many other places, has played a part in England's history. During Cromwell's time, in 1644, many of his men were stationed in the village. For providing food and shelter for one man, and food and stabling for his horse for ten days, 11 shillings was paid.

In 1620 John Howland, a resident of Fenstanton, set out from Plymouth with the Pilgrim Fathers on the *Mayflower*. They landed at Cape Cod, Massachusetts, and established the first permanent colony in New England. John Howland's mother and father lie buried in Fenstanton churchyard. In 1981 the Pilgrim John Howland Society in America gave a bell to Fenstanton church, so now there are six bells to peal out joyfully over the countryside.

In 1768 Lancelot (Capability) Brown, the famous landscape gardener, bought the manor of Fenstanton from the Earl of Northampton. Although he did not reside permanently in his manor house, he took a great deal of interest in his domain and he and his wife are both buried here.

Fenstanton is a lively village and all ages are catered for, from Brownies and Cub Scouts to senior citizens. The morris dancers tour the village on Plough Monday and bank holidays, a happy and energetic sight.

🍁 FORDHAM

Fordham lies ten miles from Ely and five miles from Newmarket, deriving its name from the ford on the river Snail, which rises two miles away in Snailwell.

There was in the Middle Ages a small Gilbertine priory, of no more than a dozen monks, near the site of the house now known as Fordham Abbey. The parish church of St Peter and St Mary Magdalene stands on slightly rising ground to the east of the river. Built between the 12th and 15th centuries, it is mainly of Early English and Decorated styles, but there are traces of Norman work and the tower, perhaps appropriately, is of the Perpendicular period. The first bells, dating from 1638, have been increased over the years, culminating in the addition of two in 1988 to make a ring of eight, and they are in constant use. Below the church a new car park leads onto the graveyard through attractive wrought iron gates erected in memory of Harry Palmer, a well-loved churchwarden and councillor. The church has two unusual features. Above the North Porch is a Lady Chapel that until the 19th century was not open to the main church. The interior of the church – chancel, nave and below the tower – is painted, the work of two sisters, Edith and Minnie Townsend, and of C.P. Leonard. There is also a painted 'window' commemorating James Reynolds Withers.

'Poet Withers' or the 'rural poet of Cambridgeshire' was born in Weston Colville, the son of a shoemaker, but lived in Fordham from a young age. He never attended school, being taught to read and write

The village sign, Fordham

by his mother. Though his poems became well known, his family was often in poverty and on one occasion Queen Victoria sent him £50. He lived by the river in Poet's Cottage where until recently a relative still lived. After his death in 1892 a public subscription raised £54 for a memorial over his grave. There is a permanent exhibition of his life and work in the village hall.

At the beginning of the 20th century the population was about 1,400; a hundred years later it is now 2,300. In the early 1990s employment was mainly in agriculture and horticulture, with the scabious being developed commercially here. Flower growing for the cut flower trade developed on a considerable scale between the wars, and Fordham's flowers became known in most of the large markets in the country. Though commercial flower growing has largely disappeared, there are two nurseries in the village and farming is still important. There is a bakery run by the third and fourth generations of one Palmer family, while another Palmer family run a farm, a milk

79

delivery and agricultural engineers. The large transport firm, Turner's, has outgrown its central village site and migrated to the southern edge of the parish on the Suffolk border, where it has been joined by David Smith's Packaging, formerly in Burwell, and the Horse Racing Forensic Laboratory from Newmarket. Still within the village are the headquarters of Allen Newport's, the sand and gravel business, and Roger Turner's Transport. There are three pubs, a post office, a butcher's, a Co-op, two garages, an electrical shop and a paper shop.

The village hall is known as the Victoria Hall, having been built to celebrate the Queen's Diamond Jubilee. A large recreation ground was given to the village by the Dunn Gardner family, formerly of Fordham Abbey. It has cricket, football and tennis pitches and a children's play area. Recently an all weather surface was added. A bowls green is adjacent. The village school was founded as a National School. Originally by the main A142 from Ely to Newmarket, it transferred to a new building opposite the church in the 1960s.

In the 19th century elections, the men of the neighbouring Isleham had to come to Fordham school to vote. Fighting often seems to have broken out, possibly because the villages had opposing political views. On one occasion the Riot Act had to be read outside the old school.

The village sign recalls King James I hunting the hare between Fordham and Chippenham in the early 17th century.

🍁 FOXTON

If you travel seven miles south on the A10 road from Cambridge you will almost certainly be stopped by the level-crossing gates at Foxton. However, the village is not on the main road. The heart of Foxton, half a mile away, is out of sight of the road and the railway. Station Road and High Street, an irregular 'T', form the skeleton of the village with occasional lanes and paths giving onto fields and farms.

There has been a settlement in Foxton since the Iron Age. Local author Rowland Parker traces 2,000 years of Foxton's history in his best-selling book *The Common Stream*. Thanks to his archaeological research and study of a mass of documentation more is known about the village's history than about that of many other villages. Even the village's name has changed over the centuries from Foxetuna in the Domesday Book to Foxtun in 1218, then it became Voxtun in 1300, Foxston in the 15th century and now Foxton, 'the farm where foxes abound'. Clunch stone, an early building material from the local hard chalk, is very much in evidence. It appears as cottage walls topped by thatch or clay tiles, in garden walls, barns and pigsties. The groups of old cottages are interspersed with farm buildings, converted pubs and newer bungalows and houses. There are also occasional terraces of turn-of the-century houses; these bear such names as Caxton, Chaucer and Byron Cottage and owe their existence to the 'Press' which stands by the war memorial at the junction of the 'T'.

The University Tutorial Press, its original title, was at first situated in East Road, Cambridge, but as it grew a larger site was needed and so in 1908 the works moved to Foxton. Today it has expanded further and is now known as The Burlington Press.

Opposite the 'Press' stands the school, built in 1833 and still a very important part of village life. For several years Foxton has awaited its replacement by a community school which will also serve as a village hall and sports pavilion. All the social life of the village with its numerous clubs and associations will be centred on this building on the recreation round. With the coming of the new school there will also be a new housing development which will inevitably change the appearance of the village.

There has been a church on the site for over a thousand years – six churches, if one considers each rebuilding as a new church. Foxton has had its share of less than worthy vicars and achieved notoriety in the 14th century when villagers violated sanctuary by dragging a murderer from the altar steps.

Despite the changes of the last thousand years Foxton remains a village surrounded by farmland. Many of the trees lost by disease or storms have been replaced and two plantations of mixed woodland have been planted south of the village for future generations.

🍁 FRIDAY BRIDGE

The name of Friday Bridge must be known in some distant corners of the world for each year many young people, from such places as Turkey, Italy and the African continent, are attracted to the Agricultural Camp on the outskirts of the village.

Perhaps on arrival they look for a bridge. As no bridge is visible they may ponder on the name. There was once a bridge but it lies as an archway beneath the road and gardens near the clock tower. The entrance to it has been sealed with concrete. A bridge suggests water. Not too much of this can be seen either!

Not so far from the village centre are the droves and the fens like Laddus Drove, Maltmas Drove, Needham, Crowmere and Waldersea Fens. These names speak of earlier times when the shepherds and herdsmen drove their sheep, cattle, goats and geese along the trackways to graze on the open fen. Nowadays little stock appears to be raised, for the drainage of the area has meant the end of serious flooding and vast expanses of flat, fertile land available for cultivation. Thus, as well as a great variety of fruit and vegetables, there are acres of wheat, barley and sugar beet surrounding the village. These open spaces make the great flocks of birds more noticeable both on land and in the air.

St Mark's church has had its lopsided look almost since its erection in 1860. The church foundations were laid on peat. As the peat dried out or was dug up from the land round about, the church began to drop. The biggest movement took place in the first 20 years of the church's existence and in the dry summer of 1921. However, the building now remains reasonably stable so folk need feel no undue alarm when visiting this friendly church!   Just over a year after the ending of the First World War the then Vicar of St Mark's, the Rev Covey Crump, stood on a lorry to pull away a Union Jack and unveil the plaque bearing the names of 24 men from the village who were killed in the war. The plaque is to be seen on the clock tower, erected as a memorial by voluntary public subscription.

One outstanding landmark is the water tower. This is a brick construction with some decoration and arched windows. It is difficult to believe it houses a gigantic tank holding some 100,000 gallons of water as it seems more like the keep of an ancient castle. From here the citizens of March, Wisbech, Chatteris and district obtain their fresh water. Under the turf beside the tower one million gallons are stored!

Two more modern buildings, not so outstanding in height, are the primary school and the community centre. The community centre was a dream come true for some public spirited villagers when it was opened in 1984, and has been renamed Tower Hall.

🍁 FULBOURN

The village of Fulbourn lies about five miles east of the city of Cambridge, at the southern edge of the fens. The name is derived from the Anglo-Saxon 'Fugelburne' meaning 'a stream frequented by birds'. The streams and open water seen here a century ago are now dried up by pumping, but a nature reserve has been established in part of the manor grounds.

In past centuries the village relied almost entirely on agriculture, but now it is more of a dormitory village for the Cambridge area. In 1851 the Electoral Register listed 311 persons eligible to vote, but in 1988 the total was 3,059 and it has risen since.

A prominent feature of the village as you approach from the city is the windmill, built in 1908 at the top of a small hill. It is said to be one of three smock mills remaining in the county and one of the finest examples of 'Dutch work' in England, with three sets of stones. In

1933 it was struck by lightning and it finally ceased working in 1936 when the fantail was blown off in a storm. It is now preserved and is gradually being restored by a local Windmill Society.

Fulbourn Manor is the most striking house in the village and is a grand 18th century (and later) replacement of a Tudor building, part of which remains as a separate dwelling house. The manor passed to Richard Greaves Townley upon the death of his mother about 200 years ago and it has remained the home of the Townley family ever since. Richard Greaves Townely was Member of Parliament for Cambridge from 1827 to 1852 and Charles Watson Townley was Lord Lieutenant of the county later in the century. The family have been great benefactors to the village.

For seven centuries the village had two parish churches standing side by side in the same churchyard, dedicated respectively to All Saints and Saint Vigor. However, in 1766 the tower of All Saints collapsed into the church and in 1775 a private Act of Parliament was obtained to allow All Saints *not* to be rebuilt and the two parishes to share St Vigor's church. Two clergymen continued to be appointed to the two parishes (as Rector of St Vigor's and Vicar of All Saints) until the appointments were united in 1876. The lychgate, erected in 1923, is one of several memorials to men of the village who fell in the First World War.

In July 1850, 47 acres of land on the Cambridgeshire side of the village were purchased for the erection of the new 'Pauper Lunatic Asylum' and the first patients arrived from the Hoxton Asylum in 1855. In 1992 it was renamed Fulbourn Hospital and saw pioneering work in the care of mentally ill people. In 1976 it housed some 700 patients; since then, 'care in the community' has greatly reduced the number of in-patients in this hospital and has led to the total closure of the neighbouring Ida Darwin Hospital for mentally handicapped people. Some patients continue to be cared for in Fulbourn Hospital and the Windmill Special School for handicapped children continues on the Ida Darwin site.

Fulbourn is an attractive village with a great mixture of old and modern houses surrounded by farmland. It has a strong community spirit, despite its size, and is well served by a good array of shops. Three public houses remain of the fourteen seen here in years gone by.

Home Close is a residential home and day centre built in 1969 and recently much renovated. The village primary school has about 250 pupils, who mostly move on to Bottisham Village College at the age of 11. The Townley Memorial Hall on the edge of the village provides good facilities for amateur dramatic and social functions, which are now supplemented by a community centre which uses part of the former infant school.

❧ GAMLINGAY

Gamlingay is rather an appealing village name and often causes speculation as to its origin. It does not mean gambolling in the hay! It is actually derived from the Saxon language and the area was known as Gamlin's Hae, which meant Gamlin's Island. This was because in those days most of the surrounding area was wet and marshy.

The Avenell family held one of the three manors in Gamlingay in 1308, and they helped with money when the rebuilding of the church took place. They held the manor for many years until the male line died out, and an Avenell daughter married into the St George family. The manor was eventually acquired by Merton College, Oxford, who still own land there today.

A more recent famous son of the parish was Squadron Leader A. H. Orlebar who captained the victorious Schneider Trophy teams in 1929 and 1931, in the latter year winning the trophy outright. In 1929 he set up a world Airspeed record of 355.80 mph.

John Bunyan used to come to preach in the village and is reputed to have founded the Baptist chapel here.

Perhaps the most momentous event in the history of Gamlingay was the Great Fire in 1660 which destroyed 76 houses and lost

Gamlingay its market which had flourished for many years.

The most important building is the parish church of St Mary the Virgin. According to Nikolaus Pevsner, it is the most impressive church in the area. In 1653 Miles Gray, the third member of the famous family of bellfounders, came to Gamlingay and cast five bells which he hung in the church tower. Three of these bells are still there today. Near the church is a splendid timber-framed house known as the Emplins. The Cock Inn is at least 400 years old.

A medieval rhyme mentions the village approvingly:

> Sutton for mutton
> Potton for beef
> Gamlingay for pretty girls
> Waresley for thieves.

🍁 THE GIDDINGS

Great Gidding is a very old village on the remote rural western boundary of the county, straddling the B660 Kimbolton to Ramsey road. The long, narrow properties at the top of the village are still known as the 'strips' from the medieval arrangement of land management. The school was founded by the Fitzwilliam family of Milton, Peterborough. The 13th century church of St Michael has an octagonal wooden plaque on its chancel wall with a Latin palindrome inscribed as a word square.

> SATOR
> ARIPO
> TENIT
> OPERA
> ROTAS

(This is thought to be a mistake; if the 'I's were 'E's it would work.)

Little Gidding is a tiny hamlet a mile south east of Great Gidding. It is widely known as the home of the Ferrar community. In 1626 Nicholas and his family, some 30 people, gave up their brilliant positions in the world to lead simple practical Christian lives there. They taught the village children, nursed the sick, wrote and bound books and three times a day walked in procession from their manor to the tiny church of St John the Evangelist in strict observance of the offices of the Book of Common Prayer. Only in this way, the Ferrars thought, could any real protest be made against the scandalous religious bickering and cruelties which preoccupied the country at that time. The experiment at Little Gidding made particular appeal to King Charles I and he stayed with the Ferrars on three different occasions, the last time as a lonely, hunted man. One of the fields nearby is known as King Charles Meadow over which it is recorded he once rode to Coppingford Grange after taking refuge from Cromwell's soldiers shortly before his capture. Some of the books written and bound by the Ferrar community are now in the British Museum. Nicholas died in 1637 and the Parliamentarian troops burnt the house and church in 1647. There is not a sign of the great house or gardens as T. S. Eliot wrote in his poem *Little Gidding*:

> 'Dust in the air suspended,
> Marks the place where a story ended'

The church was rebuilt in 1714.

In July 1937 a pilgrimage was organised by the Church Union, the organisation of the Anglo Catholics, to celebrate the 300th anniversary of the death of Nicholas Ferrar. Pilgrimages became a regular feature for several years with the meadows filled with visitors, gathered to pay homage to a man who made his faith a living force.

In 1938 Alan Maycock, an academic of Cambridge, published books about Nicholas Ferrar and the community. In his biography of Nicholas Ferrar he asked the rhetorical questions, 'Will the torch ever be relighted in this holy place? Will it ever be restored to God's greater glory and become once again a spiritual power house from which the church and her children may draw strength and inspiration?'

When he visited Little Gidding in 1946 with his wife Enid and friends, he found it in a very rundown and wretched state and wondered about forming 'The Friends of Little Gidding'. This was done on 31st July 1946 with the Bishop of Ely as president and Canon Jones, vicar of Great Gidding, as warden. During the first five years, the church was repaired and refurbished and membership grew to over 200.

In 1968 Alan Maycock died; his biography of Nicholas Ferrar was read by Robert Van de Weyer and in 1977 Robert and Sarah moved to Little Gidding to try to put the vision of Alan Maycock into practice.

This is now a modern ecumenical community, developing in the remaining buildings of the tiny hamlet and known as 'The community of Christ, the Sower'. In 1986 a second branch started, five miles away at Leighton Bromswold, based on Castle House where the Van de Weyer family now live with other young people who wish to share the life of the community for a while. Other members live in the village nearby. Robert Van de Weyer is vicar of Great and Little and Steeple Giddings, Hamerton, Winwick and Upton parishes.

🍁 GIRTON

In medieval times Girton was a typical English village, a prosperous and settled community. In 1279 the Hundred Rolls Survey gives a population of over 200. Towards the end of the Middle Ages the feudal society underwent change and so too did the names of the lords of the manor. The Trumpington family, who had owned most of the land for 300 years, faded away and new names appeared, such as the Cotton family.

The 17th century saw the drainage of the fens. The Cotton family showed great interest in agricultural experiments and consequently in the drainage of the land around Girton. Although there were some substantial yeomen tenant farmers, Girton was not a village of the wealthy at that time.

By the 18th century, craftsmen such as the tailor, blacksmith, carpenter, the carter and the thatcher appear in the village, indicating that the farmland was now more productive and could support more people. It is at this time that the Old Rectory was built by Edmund Halfhyde, Rector of Girton. This is now a language school.

In the second half of the 19th century Girton began to change more quickly. The Agricultural and Industrial Revolutions altered the nature of village society. Familiar crafts and occupations disappeared – no blacksmith appears in the registers after 1865, no thatcher after 1881 and no horse dealer after 1863. The agricultural labourers provided the backbone of the village work, but in 1899 we hear of a shunter and an engine driver.

In the early part of the 19th century a Dame School was held in a cottage in the High Street, but in 1844 a school was built next to the church by Miss Anne Marcia Cotton (later Mrs Richard Houblon), the daughter of the rector at that time, who also gave an endowment of £1,000 to pay for its upkeep and the schoolmaster's salary. The school was to be mixed. The school became State aided in 1877 against Miss Cotton's wishes.

Girton College bought a 16 acre site at the corner of Girton Road and Huntingdon Road in 1871. The new college provided accommodation for 21 students, three lecture rooms and a small dining hall. The first 15 students moved in during September 1873. The college was a source of employment for the village girls either in the laundry or kitchen.

Girton Feast Week was held during the week after Trinity. Treats included roundabouts, swing boats and stalls with brandy snaps.

In 1911 the population was still only 543. In 1921 it began to grow and was 1,112 by 1931. By 1948 the population had reached 2,139, following a great expanse of house building.

Girton, like many other villages, took its quota of evacuees during the first weeks of the Second World War. Tales of the exploits of these children include a cow being shot by a bow and arrow while 'jungle warfare' was being practised; also of the boy who stole a cattle drinking trough and successfully navigated it nearly as far as Waterbeach. A family of seven sisters demanded to be billeted together. A case of scarlet fever caused a whole family to be billeted in the Isolation Hospital on the Oakington Road but they all disappeared during the first night, back to London and civilization.

The women of Girton did their 'bit' for the war. The WI made 4 tons of jam with fruit and sugar, preserved in cans, and the salvage campaign encouraged them: 'Women of Girton – lay your bones here'. After the war more peaceful pursuits returned and the land opposite the church was secured and developed as a Memorial Garden to Alice Hibbert-Ware, a distinguished naturalist who lived here until her death in 1944.

By 1970 there were 3,000 on the electoral roll.

The City Northern Bypass, built in 1978/79, sliced through the village near Pepys Way and although in a cutting still causes concern with noise and air pollution and monitoring equipment is periodically installed on the bridge over the roadway. Despite this a housing development has gone ahead next to the bridge. At the other end of the village there is a housing development for over 55s in the High Street. A nursery school occupies the former baker's shop and, with the closure and demolition of the laundry and deep freeze, the Wellbrook Court office development now occupies the site, providing employment for several villagers.

The village has a good measure of amenities with riding stables, Littleton House School for boys, chapel, golf course, post office-cum-shop, two public houses, two nursery schools and primary school, recreation/playing fields with pavilion, two sheltered housing developments, a plant nursery and florist, allotments, purpose-built doctor's surgery, Gretton Courts flats for retired business/professional people, Women's Institute Hall, Co-op shop with extended opening hours, office development housing four business employing over a hundred people, three shops in the Thornton Road area and a half-hourly bus service to Cambridge.

Periodically the village comes under threat of being absorbed into

Cambridge, but whatever happens Girton residents will retain their community spirit.

GLATTON

Glatton, an attractive village of 105 dwellings, is situated one mile west of the new A1(M). Aptly described as 'the Village in the Valley' in the 1930s by a former resident, Beverly Nichols, it is now a mixture of traditional cottages, some from the 17th and 18th centuries, Victorian houses and modern developments, almost half the village being built since 1950. Up until then village life revolved around farming with dairy herds and pig farming predominating. Now, however, it is, like many others, mainly a commuter and retirement village.

There is an active church community centring on St Nicholas' church which dates back to the 15th century. The village hall, built in the early 1950s, is the hub of village affairs although increasingly this is a dormitory village where the majority of people do not join in local activities. Glatton is fortunate to still have a village shop and post office. The Addison Arms, an 18th century Dutch-gable-ended public house, is a favoured meeting place both for the villagers of Glatton and for those from the surrounding area.

☘ GLINTON

Glinton lies six miles north of Peterborough, just off the A15. It is a pleasant rural community with some attractive cottages and houses built of Barnack ragstone.

The lovely parish church of St Benedict, originally a chapel of ease to the parish of Peakirk, has a graceful 15th century spire with a recently restored peal of six bells. The 12th century Lady Chapel was once used as the village school. John Clare, the 19th century poet from Helpston, attended here and declared his love for Mary Joyce by carving her initials on the external stonework of the east wall. The gargoyles are worth noticing, especially on the south side where three show faces – and the fourth the opposite. The story is that when the stonemason considered himself unpaid, he completed his work in an appropriate manner!

Opposite the church is the primary school, founded in 1845. The original building and adjacent schoolhouse have been much extended over the years. The Arthur Mellows Village College, a more modern building on Helpston Road, caters for young people from Glinton and several surrounding villages. Both schools are important contributors to the community life of the village, as is the village hall, which was once the Methodist chapel.

Glinton at present has two public houses, two general stores and a butcher's. The shop in Rectory Lane formerly housed the village fire engine, convenient to the village pump, once the major source of water. The pump was in use until the Second World War. Many a child's task on returning from school each afternoon used to be to take buckets to the pump and collect the family's daily water requirements.

North Fen Lane includes some lovely old houses and leads to open fields, and despite the loss of some leafy lanes there are still pleasant walks to be enjoyed. The stone bridge half a mile down the lane was once the illicit meeting place for Mary Joyce and John Clare.

Back in the village, the 17th century house of Manor Farm betrays Dutch influence. Mary Joyce lived here and her ghost is rumoured to have been seen at the round window. There is an unsubstantiated legend of an underground passage running from Manor Farm to Peakirk.

In recent years there has been much new building, particularly on the east side of the village. Although it has become a dormitory for Peterborough, and even for London, there are still some older residents who have lived and worked in the neighbourhood all their lives, and the community spirit continues to thrive.

☘ THE GRANSDENS

Great and Little Gransden are only a few hundred yards apart and the churches of both can be seen from The Dole field which separates the villages.

Many changes have taken place over the years. Before the Second World War it was predominantly a farming community but wartime brought the Gransden Lodge airfield, part of which is now home to the Cambridge University Gliding Club. In Great Gransden church there is a stained glass window commemorating the 801 airmen of 405 Squadron of the Royal Canadian Air Force who gave their lives in 1941–45.

Great Gransden still has its village school, Barnabas Oley Church of England Primary. This was started by the Royalist vicar of the same name in 1670 and has continued ever since at various sites in the village. It is reputed to be about the oldest primary school in the country and now boasts new buildings attached to the earlier Victorian one.

There is also a restored 17th century post windmill with the carved date '1614'. The mill last worked in 1911.

The Reading Room was created by Theodore Vincent Webb in 1871. He was also responsible for the building of the Victorian school. Today the attractive thatched reading room holds the meetings of many of the thriving groups and societies in the village. Little Gransden, although a smaller village, has a larger village hall which is used for bigger functions and sports.

The village is lucky enough to have a village stores and post office where you can still buy Zebrite black-leading alongside the more modern necessities of life like Taco Shells and Smokey Bacon crisps!

The villages have many thatched properties, some with interesting histories, but over recent years these have new neighbours in modern properties. The influx of people into the villages has brought the population back to that of earlier this century and helps the village to thrive, but everyone hopes that the villages will not grow too much and lose their character.

❧ GRANTCHESTER

The parish is bounded on two sides by water. To the south is the Bourn Brook, running from the west to Byron's Pool. At Byron's Pool, also called Old Mills, the brook joins the river Cam, also called the Granta and Rhee or Rea. This river is the parish's eastern boundary down to Newnham.

The history of the river is nearly all the history of its mills. In the Domesday Book two mills are mentioned and it is possible there was one at Byron's Pool and another at Newnham. They were both worth 40 shillings and 'half a wier half a thousand eels'. It was said the best time for catching eels was after a thunderstorm when the river was full and muddy. One man is supposed to have sold enough eels to buy his granddaughter a grand piano! There is no mill in Grantchester now; the last one was destroyed by fire on 30th October 1928.

The parish church of St Andrew and St Mary stands on a slight rise in the middle of the village. It is in the living of Corpus Christi College, Cambridge. It consists of a 14th century chancel and a 15th century tower and nave. When a south aisle was added in 1875, remains of what are believed to have been Saxon grave-covers were found, which point to the very early existence of a church upon this site. The bowl of the font would appear to be Norman. It is made of Purbeck stone and is very large, 30 inches in diameter. Both its size and simple form give an indication of its early date. During repairs in 1875, a doorway was discovered in the north wall of the nave.

The village has been made world famous by Rupert Brooke and his poem, *The Old Vicarage, Grantchester*. The present owner of the Old Vicarage is Jeffrey Archer, Lord Archer, the author and politician. Grantchester must be the only village in the rather unusual position of having three vicarages. The first was the Old Vicarage, the second, situated in Vicarage Drive is now a private home called Glebe House and the third is next to the church where the present vicar lives.

GREAT & LITTLE CHISHILL

Great and Little Chishill are located on the southernmost tip of Cambridgeshire, with Essex about a mile to the east and Hertfordshire about a mile to the west. Until 1895, Chishill was in Essex but then the boundary was changed and it became Cambridgeshire. However, the church is still in the Chelmsford diocese and the postcode is Stevenage, Hertfordshire – very confusing for everyone! Great Chishill has the distinction of being the highest point in Cambridgeshire at 480 feet above sea level.

It is a very ancient settlement; to the north of the village runs Icknield Way and to the west is the Cumberton Brook which was the division between the Kingdom of Mercia and the Kingdom of the East Saxons. The Domesday Book of 1086 refers to Cishella, which was held by Ulfeih, a freeman, and Little Cishella, which was held by Sired, a freeman. William the Conqueror, Duke of Normandy, crowned on Christmas Day 1066 in Westminster Abbey, bestowed large pieces of England on his fellow Normans and Cishella went to Henry de Farers and Little Cishella went to Count Eustace of Boulogne.

Great Chishill was divided into five 'Maners': the Maner of Cardens, alias Bassets Hall, the Maner of Belknaps, the Maner of Tewes alias Lisles, the Maner of Friers, alias Chishall Grange, and the Maner of Chishall, alias Over Chishall-Hall. A farmhouse, Hall Farm, still occupies this latter site today, on the east side of the village.

St Swithin's church, situated on high ground at the crossroads was founded in 1136, but almost certainly there would have been a place of worship there before with the position of Deep Well House just behind it. Wells, springs, high ground and ash trees were always places of deep religious significance. The church has had a chequered

Chishill post mill

history of partly collapsing and being rebuilt over the generations. The five bells were rung for the first time in 23 years on 12th September 1998 as the beginning of a village project to get them and the bell tower repaired in time to ring in the new millennium.

Little Chishill has the church of St Nicholas, probably founded around the same time.

On 22nd February 1789 a fire broke out in the vestry house of the Congregational church in Barley Road and quickly spread throughout the village, destroying many houses and setting light to the tower of St Swithin's – but no lives were lost. The Congregational church was first built in 1694 and rebuilt in 1894.

The Chishill post mill stands to the west of the village on the road to Barley. The first authenticated record of a mill here appears in 1592 though it is possible there was one before. The first recorded owners were the Cooke family and the first recorded miller was Joseph Rule in 1677. The Cambridgeshire County Council acquired

96

the mill in the 1960s, after William Pegram stopped working it in 1951. It is now preserved and open to the public.

In 1886 (*Kelly's Directory of Essex*) the village was alive with tradesmen, bakers, butchers, wheelwrights, bricklayers, dressmakers, six farms in Great Chishill and one in Little Chishill, with their attendant labourers, two public houses – the White Horse and the Plough (now the Pheasant) – a shop and post office and the village school for a hundred children. All that has now gone – the shop closed in the late 1970s and the school in 1971. There is now only St Swithin's church, the United Reform church, the Pheasant, a playing field and sports pavilion and a very fine village hall built in 1982. However, two farms are still being worked in Great Chishill and one in Little Chishill.

In the 1991 census profile of Great and Little Chishill parish, there were 237 dwellings and a population of 634. The villages are fortunate in having a fairly balanced mix of old and new houses with varied architecture, some of the oldest houses being in Maltings Lane, off May Street, where once the Quakers used to meet.

A significant claim to fame is an entry in the *Guinness Book of Records* – on 10th September 1983 Ben Palmer, a local farmer, and Owen North, the local baker, produced loaves of bread from wheat in the field in 40 minutes and 44 seconds.

🍁 GREAT PAXTON

Situated three miles to the north of the market town of St Neots, Great Paxton is approached over a hill with pleasant sweeping views of the river Great Ouse and the Ouse valley which lies to the west of the village. The railway embankment runs through the fields between the river and the village.

The village today has changed from thatched cottages, a small council estate and surrounding farms to a large village with nearly 400 houses. There is a new, expanding primary school, a shop and post office, a community room and a pub called the Bell. Once there was another pub called the Black Bull but this was converted to a house a long while ago, as was the Towgood Institute. More recently the tiny Victorian school and schoolhouse have been converted into a modern home. Other additions to the village include the recreation ground and sports pavilion for local football and cricket teams, and a fine children's playground on Saxon Green. There are many thriving clubs and societies of all kinds in the village.

The church, the Minster Church of the Holy Trinity, stands out as a remarkable building dating back to about 1020. It is specifically mentioned in the Domesday Book, and is said to be one of the oldest in England. The outside appears mostly 15th century but once inside one sees the imposing Saxon church, with its pillars and arches opening onto the aisle, quite unlike anything existing in England but similar to types found on the Continent.

🍁 GREAT SHELFORD

> 'Folks in Shelford and those parts
> Have twisted lips and twisted hearts'

These malicious words by Rupert Brooke have brought fame to Great Shelford throughout the world but few people know exactly where it is! It lies on the A1301, south of Cambridge. Shelford was first mentioned in the 11th century under the name of Scelford (shallow ford). In 1279 there were about 105 houses and 38 landholders.

The common land in Great Shelford was enclosed in 1835 after which 64% of the land belonged to Gonville and Caius, St John's and Jesus Colleges. The remainder was divided among smaller owners.

In 1845 the railway to Cambridge was opened and Shelford had its own station. The railway led to more building which still continues. The M11 motorway was opened in 1980 with an access less than one mile from the village.

The population of Shelford is mainly professional, some working in local small firms. The Alzheimer's Research Trust is housed in Litvanos House built in 1870. Many people travel to the village to work in modern office blocks. The village has excellent shopping and parking facilities. It has its own Health Care Centre and there are many community and social organisations.

The church of St Mary was largely rebuilt about 1400 but includes features from the 12th, 13th and 14th centuries. The spire was blown down in 1703 and was restored in 1843, 1931 and 1985. There is a Doom painting of about 1400 on the chancel arch. The chancel screen is 15th century. The parish register survives from 1557. There is a very active Baptist chapel in High Street.

Little Shelford shares the Church of England primary school which dates from 1843. In 1870 a school was built for Nonconformists at the junction of Woollards Lane and Church Street; this is now used as a garage. It is said that there were many 'brainy' schoolchildren in Great Shelford during the 19th century. The University dons were not allowed girl friends within four miles of their colleges. Great Shelford is exactly four miles!

Some interesting old houses are to be found in Shelford. Several are thatched and one in Church Street may have been a guildhall in the early 16th century. There are three public houses. All have a good history and a brisk trade!

🍁 GREAT STAUGHTON

Great Staughton is divided into three distinct parts, the Highway, the Town and the moor, all of which conceal a surprisingly rich and varied history, beginning with a settlement in Neolithic times.

The Highway straddles the B645 and is noted for the famous sundial dating from 1637 and the White Hart, a 17th century coaching inn. However, the historic heart of the village is the Town, which lies about half a mile from the sundial along a minor road leading to Little Staughton. The Town is dominated by two celebrated buildings: the church of St Andrew that dates from the 13th century and Place House, built in 1539.

In 1958/9 a substantial winged-corridor-type Roman villa was excavated to the south of Staughton. Hoards of coins found allowed the archaeologists to date the site to AD 130–370. Great Staughton was also mentioned in the Domesday Book in 1086 under the name of Tochestone and was a village of some importance whose ownership was disputed between the Bishop of Lincoln and Ramsey Abbey.

Apart from the historic sundial and the White Hart, today the Highway is home to a post office, a much-used garage, a butcher and an extremely friendly medical practice.

The minor road leading to the church will also take you to the primary school and an entrance to the sports pavilion, opened in 1996 by the then Prime Minister John Major. Following the B645 around the bend and heading towards Kimbolton, you reach the well-used village hall. A little further on, sustenance can be found at the Tavern.

On the Moor there is a small but thriving industrial site offering varied employment.

Great Staughton has slowly grown since the 1970s and forms a well integrated community, with over twenty clubs and associations to satisfy most needs an d a very informative village magazine which goes to all households free every month – so whilst not warranting the adjective 'pretty', it is nevertheless a thriving, caring village.

🍁 GREAT STUKELEY

Great Stukeley is situated on the B1042 just 2 miles north of Huntingdon. The village can boast the usual amenities – a public house, an old country inn, a post office, two churches, a playing field, a village hall, one of the oldest Women's Institutes in the country, dating from just after the First World War, and, oh yes, John Major, the former Prime Minister.

St Bartholomew's church dates back to the 13th century with records that can be seen on request. The inn dates back to the 16th century and is situated beside the old Roman road. Further evidence of the Romans can be found in the form of two tumuli (Roman burial grounds) on each side of the road, one of which is in the playing field and the other opposite the village hall.

🍁 GREAT WILBRAHAM

Great Wilbraham was an important place in early times, situated as it was on a narrow belt of firm land between marshes and dense forest, through which the Romans launched their attack on Boadicea and later, in the 7th century, King Penda's Midland Federation marched against East Anglia. The great earthwork, Fleam Dyke, is a reminder of these stirring times. The victorious Penda bestowed the land behind the dyke on his daughter, Wilburh, and she, in turn, gave her name to the village: Wilburgaham – 'Wilburh's homestead'.

One of the oldest tracks in England, the Streetway, passes through the parish and excavations in the area have revealed evidence that there was a Roman settlement there before Wilburh's time.

In the 13th century the manor of Great Wilbraham was acquired by the Knights Templars. In the 14th century the Templars fell into disgrace and the Wilbraham manor passed to their rivals, the Knights Hospitallers. The house on the site of the preceptory is known as the Temple to this day and one of its outbuildings, dating from the 15th century, was probably part of the private apartments of a commander of the Hospitallers.

After Henry VIII's suppression of religious orders Great Wilbraham had a measure of independence under absentee landlords and the village was run by its leading farming families, the Olivers, the Ballards and the Smiths. Perhaps it was this independent spirit which made Great Wilbraham a centre of Nonconformity in the

The dovecote at Great Wilbraham

17th century. Behind Crossways (originally Cross Farm) in the High Street is a small Nonconformist graveyard where members of the Webb, Paul and Dennis families are buried.

The last decades of the 18th century saw great changes in the village when the Hicks family moved into the Temple and bought up much of the farmland. The villagers retained the common on which they could graze one cow or two yearling calves. Many householders in the village still enjoy these common rights.

The Hicks family took a great interest in the welfare of the villagers. Most of the cottages belonged to their estate and most of the men worked on the land, so life revolved around the 'Big House'. Under the spell of this vigorous paternalism Great Wilbraham remained out of the modern world until the Second World War when an American airfield was built nearby and tanks were stationed in the Temple park. Even in the early 1960s most of the older inhabitants of the village worked on the land and a newspaper article of the time records that 'the whole rhythm of village life is dependent

102

on the harvest and the sowing'.

It was the advent of mains drainage in the early 1970s which really opened the village up to new building, but luckily only 'infilling' has been allowed and on the whole the new houses blend harmoniously with the old cottages and the village remains a close and friendly community.

In the 1990s the village acquired a new school, a development of 16 houses called 'Squire's Field' in memory of Squire Hicks and a very attractive village sign which depicts several facets of village history. On the sign Wilburh is seated in state at the centre with the village church beside her; within a medallion in the foreground two knights are riding a single horse (a device of the Knights Templars) and in the background the agricultural tradition of the village is represented by wheat, barley and sugarbeet. A hare, pheasant, a fieldmouse and some poppies complete the design.

🍁 GUILDEN MORDEN

Guilden Morden, once described as Golden Morden, lies in the pleasantly undulating country south west of Cambridge, near the Bedfordshire border and close to Hertfordshire. It was mentioned in the Domesday Book as the 'other' Morden – alia Mordum – to differentiate it from its close neighbour, Steeple Morden, which at the time was slightly less populous.

In 1871 there were a little over 1,000 people living in the village, the last increase resulting from the prosperity which came to Guilden Morden with the digging of coprolite. This was a phosphate dug as an early fertilizer but the industry died with imports from Chile. Consequently the population fell and in 1931, 60 years later, the population had dropped to 533. Now this quiet village is once again becoming a sought-after place in which to live. In common with most local villages there were a large number of public houses from the 19th century. Though there are only two remaining open, the

Parish pump, Guilden Morden

Edward VII in Trap Road and the Three Tuns in the High Street, many older residents can still name at least nine. They can also recall a butcher's shop, two bakeries, the last one, Lindsays, closing in 1976, and they remember small grocer's and sweet shops. In April 1998, sadly, the general store and post office was closed as a buyer could not be found.

Until the mid 1970s, Guilden Morden was one of the only villages in the district to have a farrier. When Mr Oswald Kaye died the forge closed and the nameplate on the house in Church Street indicates where it was situated.

No story about Guilden Morden would be complete without a mention of St Mary's church, built on the highest point in the village with a splendid tower and lofty spire, a feature of the neighbourhood. St Mary's was begun in the 13th century and was in its present form in the 15th, though according to history there was certainly a church of some kind there soon after the Norman Conquest. There has also been a suggestion that it was built on an earlier religious site.

Other notable features of the church are the parclose or rood screen and the clock. The screen has survived intact and research into church woodwork indicates that of its date it is the finest of its kind in the country. According to records the clock, with no minute hand, is said to be one of the best preserved of tower clocks in the neighbourhood. After St Mary's church bells had been silent for some eight months and following the massive fundraising efforts in the village, the six bells were lowered in March 1992 by volunteers from the RAF base at Henlow and taken to Loughborough for restoration. In October they were restored and two new ones hung. An offer from John Gypson of Meldreth to make fittings and hang the two new bells, one donated by the villagers of nearby Wendy, made it possible for the eight bells to be hung in the oak frame designed for the purpose in 1877.

There has been an Independent Congregational chapel in the village for about a century and a half. The handsome building in Pound Green was closely associated with the Rev Joseph Stockbridge who founded and continued as its pastor for 50 years.

The village is proud of its modern Church of England primary school in Pound Green where there are 61 pupils. The school was officially opened by the Bishop of Ely in 1975, though the children moved from the old school in Church Street in 1974. The old school built in 1846 is now a private residence.

There are a lot of old houses and cottages in Guilden Morden, a few of them thatched. Among the older properties is the fine manor house of Morden Hall in Trap Road. It stands on a moated site and has its own chapel. On Avenells in Church Street is the date 1680 but the house has been restored and enlarged over the years.

Guilden Morden is proud of its village sign standing on the Green at the junction of Church Street and Church Lane, unveiled in December 1997 by the then oldest inhabitant, Mr Leslie Huffer.

✤ HADDENHAM

Haddenham is the highest and the most southern village in the Isle of Ely. As the village is 116 feet above sea level and is surrounded by the low-lying fens it is a very noticeable feature of the landscape. Because of its position, Haddenham was a well-known settlement long before the fens were drained.

During recent years excavations in the fen at Hillrow have unearthed a Roman settlement and a Neolithic megalith in a long barrow. As the latter is the first, and at the moment the only, wooden mortuary structure to be found intact, the 6,000 year old mausoleum is a particularly exciting find. The mausoleum, which is 6 metres long and 1½ metres wide, is housed in the British Museum, and it is hoped that a replica being constructed will be housed in nearby Denney Abbey.

On the site of the one-time Haddenham Gas Company, brickyard and pits is now an established lake, naturalised garden and wildlife sanctuary. This important conservation area, covering some five acres, has come into the ownership of the Parish Council, to ensure its preservation.

The village has several old houses and at the top of the hill stands the church of Holy Trinity. Legend has it that the first church in Haddenham was founded by St Etheldreda and her steward Ovin, possibly in the year AD 673. Etheldreda established the monastery at Ely and it is likely that Haddenham came under its pastoral care. Etheldreda was the daughter of Anna, King of the East Angles, and was born at Exning near Newmarket and had received the Isle of Ely as a dowry on her marriage in AD 652. The present church is late 13th century and 14th century, with a major restoration in 1876, its basic structure being rubblestone and limestone with leaded roofs and end parapets with 19th century gable crosses. The carved wooden altar in the Lady Chapel is Elizabethan in origin and the font is 15th century, an interesting octagonal limestone bowl with

Holy Trinity church, Haddenham

carving. The church is a delightful setting for many occasions, particularly for the 'Flowers and Paintings' weekend held each July.

Next to the church is the Arkenstall Village Centre, so named because it was previously the school, founded by Robert Arkenstall in 1723. This building was converted into what can only be described as the very hub of village life. Village organisations use the centre, folk from a wide area come here, a Day Centre for the elderly is held twice a week, providing hot meals, entertainment and, more important, company for those living alone, and the County Library is housed in the former School House, all in all a very important asset to Haddenham.

From 1969 to 1992 Haddenham had its very own Farmland Museum based in a garden and buildings in the High Street. The bulk of the collection is now part of the Farmland Museum of Cambridgeshire, housed in the farmyard of Denny Abbey, seven miles away. Artefacts of local interest, together with educational material, form the Haddenham Bygones Collection in a portakabin at the Arkenstall Centre.

Travelling south, visitors leave the village, passing the spot where Ovin's Cross stood before being taken to Ely Cathedral. In about ¼ mile is the recently found Quaker burial ground and the renovated remains of the last of the village's windmills. On the right is a red brick house which is unusual inasmuch as the bricks used in its construction were baked on the site.

And so to Aldreth, a small hamlet with a Baptist chapel. Here the houses run right to the edge of the fens and only farm roads continue from the village. Here the waters of the 1947 floods lapped dangerously close.

If travellers approach the village from the west they will be immediately aware of North Hill which gives some of the finest views of the fens. This is Hillrow and has a terrace of houses built to accommodate Dutch drainage workers. These men were most unpopular locally as by draining the fens they totally altered the lifestyle of the fen people, whose livelihood was founded on fishing and wildfowling. The same Dutch engineers are believed to have built the oldest house in Haddenham, the Porch House, which has 1657 inscribed over the front porch.

Approaching the village centre, visitors pass the village green with its fine, locally crafted village sign. It is bordered by the manor house and the Baptist chapel on one side and the Old Baptist Hall and burial ground on the other; the latter two have become a new Health Centre and children's play area respectively.

🍁 HARDWICK

The village of Hardwick is situated about five miles west of Cambridge, just north of the ancient track called 'Portway', and is the nucleus of a parish of 1,438 acres. The earliest written record of

Hardwick dates from AD 991 when the manor of Hardwick was given to the monks of Ely by the chieftain Brithnoth or Beorhtnoth in recognition of the hospitality his army received when marching into Essex to fight the Danes. It is accepted that the name Hardwick originates from the old English 'herd' meaning herd or flock and 'wic' meaning dwelling or village and that Hardwick was originally an outlying shepherds' settlement subordinate to Toft. The soil is heavy boulder clay and despite the origins of its name, the land around Hardwick has generally been and still is more suited to arable farming than the keeping of livestock.

The See of Ely was created in 1109 and the manor of Hardwick was eventually converted for the Bishop's use. Bishop Matthew Wren, uncle to Sir Christopher Wren, finally endowed the manor of Hardwick to Pembroke College, Cambridge to enable its newly completed chapel, designed by his nephew, to be kept in good repair.

The small parish church of St Mary is a simple building consisting of nave, chancel, west tower with spire, small porch and modern vestry. It is built of field stones in the Perpendicular style dating from the late 14th or 15th century. However, a Decorated window on the south side of the chancel indicates an earlier stone building. In fact there is a reference to a church at Hardwick dated 1217. In 1858 medieval mural drawings were discovered on the south wall of the church, some of which have recently been re-exposed. The relatively complete registers date from 1569. Records frequently refer to the poor state of repair of the church. For example in 1836 the numerous holes in the roof provided ventilation but also admitted sparrows to the services! The interior of the church is currently undergoing restoration by members of the congregation. Since 1966 the rector of Hardwick has also served the parishes of Toft and Caldecote.

There is a record of a dame school at Hardwick in 1789. Following the Elementary Education Act of 1870, a new schoolroom and schoolhouse was built which opened in 1872. This was sited on glebe land near the church and cost £452, financed largely by private subscription. This school was closed in 1968 and for a few years there was no school in Hardwick. However, to meets the needs of a rapidly expanding population, a new Community Primary School was opened in 1979.

For centuries Hardwick was a totally agricultural community centred around the church and village green, with a small population fluctuating with the prosperity of farming on the relatively infertile soil. Since 1900 the village has gradually changed. The village smithy and bakehouse have gone and in the 1930s and 1940s several houses were built along the Cambridge to St Neots road about half a mile from the centre of the village. From 1970, however, several hundred houses have been built so that the parish now has about 890 households with a population of 2,240. There is a public house, two shops and a post office and several small businesses. Consequently, although the village is still completely surrounded by farmland, apple orchards and woodland, it is now very much a dormitory village for Cambridge.

🍁 HARSTON

Harston lies some five miles from Cambridge, in the valley of the Cam or Rhee. The name of the village has evolved from different spellings, the closest to present day usage being Hares-town; this and surrounding villages eg Fox-town and Hawkes-town, are said to have been the hunting ground of Queen Elizabeth I. There is evidence to suggest that Harston is of Saxon origin, but Roman as well as Saxon pottery has been found in the surrounding area.

The village is situated on the busy A10 road. It has been said that Harston 'is one long street', but with recent building developments this is now less so. The 'long street' was always bustling with travellers from Cambridge to London in wagons, carts and coaches and the inns catered for passengers and traders of all kinds. One of the oldest inns, the Coach (or Wagon) and Horses is possibly a 16th century house, and was recorded in 1800. It has been practically rebuilt, and is now a private dwelling.

At the entrance to the village, approached from Cambridge, on the High Street, stands a public house the Old English Gentleman, newly built in 1839 and named for the then rector of Fowlmere: at the opposite end of the street, where stands the war memorial, is the Pemberton Arms built around 1865. In between these two points the present day traveller will find the village stores and post office, an antique shop, garages, car showrooms etc, replacing among other things the wheelwright's shop and the smithy.

The manor house is of 17th century origin, but was extensively remodelled in the 18th and 19th centuries. Beside the manor is the parish church of All Saints. The building, built of field stones and ashlar dressing, is mostly mid to late 14th century, but there is some evidence of an earlier church on the site. The church was restored in 1853. The wooden pulpit is an example of medieval craftsmanship; the octagonal font is 15th century.

Turning on to the road to Haslingfield and bearing left, we come to a popular riverside walk. It was here in 1645 that a force of King Charles' cavalry attempted to fight their way across the river Rhee. A bloody battle ensued and the crossing was held by Cromwell's men. The site is known as The Red Field. The watermill in the vicinity dates from 1086. In the 1960s it was bought by an animal feed company and it has now undergone an architectural award-winning transformation to become the headquarters of a scientific company.

Winding north from the church is Button End, a narrow lane, partly residential, partly industrial. In 1870 it was the site of the digging of coprolites, involving an influx of 55 immigrant workers.

The village sign is situated on the (now diminished) green. It depicts a rook, a honey skip and water springs, the last recalling the beautiful clear water which welled up at many points in the village, to be collected by the people.

HARTFORD

The earliest settlement in this stretch of the river Ouse was Hartford – older than nearby Huntingdon and Godmanchester. The Saxons called it Hereforde meaning 'army ford', and it is recorded under this name in the Domesday Book. The village was originally along the banks of the river which was the main form of transport, but now it has expanded to the north and west linking up with the Borough of Huntingdon.

Church Lane leads to the church and river. The cottage which stands facing the river was originally the Anchor Inn and in 1275 a waterwheel was constructed there. Nearby in the meadow in the 13th century, St Giles' Hospital was built.

The parish church of All Saints, over 800 years old, is built on the north bank of the river, surrounded by a well-maintained churchyard with colourful flower beds overlooking peaceful meadows. This picturesque setting inspires not only local couples, but many outside the parish, to wed in the church. A family of inquisitive swans are often part of the wedding photographs.

About a mile further downstream lies the Hartford Marina, full of luxury craft for those wishing to enjoy a holiday afloat. Formerly a series of gravel pits, it now has direct access to the river by a purpose-built channel, and was given an award for its pleasing landscape transformation.

Returning to the village and wishing to quench your thirst, what better way than with a refreshing pint at one of the two local hostelries. The King of the Belgians (formerly King of the Prussians) is situated in that part of Main Street which happily is now bypassed by Longstaff Way and the roar of today's traffic. In 1964 workmen digging near the King of the Belgians public house unearthed a hoard of 1,108 French and English coins dated between 1450 and 1503. The silver coins, many in mint condition, were removed to the British Museum. A little more modern in age is the Barley Mow, with a mansard roof, built around 1804 with masonry from the remains of St Benet's church in Huntingdon.

Hartford House was built in 1730. This is a red brick house and was held in 1822 by Richard Bateman. The great features of the house are the 1730 curved staircase and the panelling in the hall and dining room. The grounds go down to the river. The manor house opposite is half-timbered, built probably by Robert Taylor, lord of the manor, who died in 1608.

A shopping parade serves the more recently developed part of the village and includes a post office, fruit and vegetable shop, newsagent and fish and chip shop, although a new supermarket within easy reach has affected local shopping habits. Nearby are situated the infant and junior schools, built to cater for the rising population, whose pupils move on to comprehensive schools in Huntingdon. In the older part of the village is another small grocery store and hairdressing salon. The social centre of the community is the village hall where numerous activities take place.

HAUXTON

Visitors to Hauxton may well think that it is a comparatively new village with an ever-expanding factory at one end and new housing estates at the other. However, nothing could be further from the truth. The Beaker Folk, Bronze Age people, settled in the area by the present-day mill, where the river Cam could be forded. It is probable that there has been a mill since Roman times, and the mill at 'Havochestun' was certainly mentioned in the Domesday Book. Over the centuries the nearby farmers brought their corn there to be ground, but the mill's heyday was in the late 18th century when it was also used for crushing coleseed (rape) for oil. In addition, the managers traded corn, coal, pitch and tar, and brick and timber for building. At that time six passenger coaches a day plied between Cambridge and London and would stop at the two alehouses, the

Ship and the Chequers, close by the mill.

Following a disastrous fire in 1851, the present mill was built. It continued to grind corn until 1974 when the last miller, Mr Maurice Turner, retired. It then passed into the hands of the nearby agrochemical factory and, sadly, now stands idle. The Old Mill House, a handsome Georgian house, and the new Mill House, built early in the 20th century, are no longer lived in and the old Mill Farmhouse and cottages have been demolished to make way for the expansion of the factory.

The parish church of St Edmund also has an ancient history. The present building was erected in the early 12th century and it is believed that a little wooden church stood on the site for about 150 years before that. So, in 1969, the village celebrated the church's millennium with a week of special services, concerts and plays, culminating in a pageant depicting the history of the church.

In 1870, led by the then vicar, the people of Hauxton were able to provide a school for the children. This handsome building served the community for over a century until, in 1971, the school was threatened with closure. The villagers strongly opposed this proposal and, instead, a new school was built and the village was able to purchase the old school building. Following alterations, it reopened in 1977 – Jubilee Year – as the village hall.

During the First World War some local men were employed in digging for coprolites – fossilised dinosaur droppings! – which made excellent fertilizer.

Before the Second World War many of the men of Hauxton worked on the land, but, with changes in farming which have taken place over the past 50 years, very few do so now.

In the 1950s people passing through the village might have seen a young bull from the local farm being taken for a walk along Church Road. On Sunday mornings he was taken for his weekly treat – a half a pint at the King's Head!

🍁 HELPSTON

Helpston is situated on the edge of the fens, about seven miles north west of Peterborough, with a population of about 800.

It is an attractive village with a large number of old buildings constructed of the local grey stone with collyweston roofs. The attractiveness of the centre of the village has been recognised by its designation as a Conservation Area. It has a long history dating back at least as far as the 12th century, although there are no records of it in the Domesday Book. The Butter Cross at the core of the village is 14th century. Its heart-shaped base is supposed to represent the Heart of Christ and a market was held there during the 16th and 17th centuries.

Helpston is most widely known as the birthplace of John Clare, the so-called 'Peasant Poet' who lived from 1793 to 1864. The primary school is named after him and there is a John Clare memorial, dated 1869, at the village centre.

Few people work in the village, most going to Stamford, Peterborough or, indeed, London. However there are several farming families who still work the surrounding land. The paper mills which were founded in the 19th century employed 230 people in 1978, but the numbers have now dropped considerably.

🍁 HEMINGFORD ABBOTS

Hemingford Abbots is a small, picturesque riverside village dating back to AD 974. It is situated between the historic market towns of Huntingdon and St Ives.

The lovely church of St Margaret of Antioch is well preserved and maintained, parts of it dating back to the 12th century. There are many desirable properties in the village, a number of which are thatched, and countless beautiful gardens. The attractive Axe and

Compass pub occupies a prominent position in the centre of the village.

Although the Peace Memorial Playing Fields are situated just over the border into Hemingford Grey they are jointly owned and administered by both Hemingfords and are, as the name implies, a lasting memorial to those villagers who gave their lives in both World Wars.

The annual Regatta is combined with Hemingford Grey and remains the only amateur regatta in the country today.

A popular walk with residents is across the meadows to Houghton and, if desired, one can continue on through the Thicket to St Ives. Hemingford Grey is but a short distance away, making a very pleasant riverside walk and a favourite rendezvous for fishermen and the small children who love to feed the ducks and swans and admire the large numbers of Brent geese which winter on the meadows beyond. Although the days of point-to-point races on the Common – at the far end of Common Lane – have long since past (due to the excavation of sand and gravel) it is still possible to walk to Godmanchester via this route.

🍁 HEMINGFORD GREY

This delightful rural village lies one and a half miles to the south west of St Ives, on the banks of the river Ouse. Owned originally by Ramsey Abbey in 1041, the village and lands of 'Hemmingforde' eventually passed into the ownership of Reginald de Grey and his successors, and thereafter from the 14th century was known as Hemingford Grey.

The village has many picturesque and historic buildings, the most interesting of these being the old manor house. Originally a stone Norman hall, built by Payn de Hemingford in the 12th century, it has since had many additions in varying styles. The original moat surrounds the house on three sides, with attractive gardens stretching to the river bank on the fourth. Believed to be the oldest inhabited house in England, it is presently occupied by the family of the famous children's authoress, the late Lucy M. Boston.

The High Street, which is in the heart of the village, offers an interesting variety of period buildings, from Glebe Cottage, a timber-framed thatched cottage dating from 1583, to the attractive yellow brick River House, which was built in the late 18th century.

Also situated in the High Street are two small shops, the village post office, the church rooms and the Reading Room. Last but not least comes the Cock Inn which has served the villagers since 1767.

At the end of the High Street lie the river and the River Walk, which affords the most delightful views across green meadowland towards Houghton, and the distant spires of St Ives' and Hemingford Abbots' churches. Standing on the river bank at the bend in the river, is the attractive 12th century St James's church, presenting one of the most beautiful and tranquil scenes to be found in the area. Adjacent to the church is Hemingford Grey House, built in 1697. Once the rectory, it is now a conference centre.

For the keen naturalists and bird watchers, there is the Marsh Lane Walk Society, a group which was formed at the instigation of the Parish Council to conserve and improve the reclaimed gravel pits on the southern boundary of the village. After much hard work by the Society, and co-operation from Redlands, the gravel pit owners, this area now forms an attractive lake, with a pleasant perimeter walk. It is renowned for the many resident and migratory wildfowl and birds which make use of the natural habitat.

An annual event worthy of note is the Hemingford Regatta, which, while not as famous as Henley, is nevertheless a very popular and pleasurable day out. It has been held on this stretch of the river since 1909 and is believed to be the last event of this kind in the country to still use ordinary pleasure boats rather than racing craft.

✹ HILDERSHAM

Hildersham is an attractive unspoilt village on the banks of the Granta (which becomes the Cam) lying about nine miles south east of Cambridge, with a population of some 200.

Hildersham was also once a Roman camp, one of many between Colchester and the North. The meadow behind the church, known as Dovehouse Meadow, has yielded Roman coins and pottery and exposed Roman foundations.

Hildersham may have been founded by Hildric, but today it owes its beautiful wooded appearance to a Victorian family, the Goodwins, who endowed both the village and the church with many treasures. Magnificent beech trees surround the parish, especially to the south of the river, whilst the Austrian pines, mainly north of the river, were brought in by the Reverend Goodwin and were at that time a rarity. They are now over 150 years old, but sadly many of them, especially the beeches, were lost in the violent storm of October 1987.

Hildersham is notable as being the last village in England in which the medieval system of stripfields was abolished and the common lands enclosed in the year 1886, some 150 years after the first Act of Enclosure. A further event occurred in 1886 – the iron bridge over the Granta in the middle of the village was built by the local blacksmith, commissioned by the Goodwin family. In fact, the blacksmith's shop remained open until 1940 on Forge Green (opposite the Pear Tree Inn) where a plaque now stands to mark its position. The Goodwins also straightened the river and if you stand on the bridge you can make out the course of the original river to the east and the west – always the first parts to flood!

Hildersham has a large area of common land, some of which is used by local farmers, but most is available to villagers and visitors just to enjoy, which is one of Hildersham's greatest assets.

Hildersham's church, The Holy Trinity, was founded in 1150. The oldest surviving portions – the vaulted sacristy and western tower –

The skeleton brass in Hildersham church

date from the early 13th century. The church has many special features and there are some well-known brasses in the floor of the chancel aisle, including three of the Paris family who provided the best Latin chronicler of the 13th century, by the name of Matthew Paris. The fourth brass is of a shroud skeleton of a man which dates from 1530. Close observers will note that there is a keyhole shape cut into this brass which dates from the time it was hung on the church door to frighten away body-snatchers (or so the story goes!).

The church is very rare inasmuch as the whole interior of the chancel, including roof, walls, window frames and mullions, was decorated in 1890 with stencilled floral work and painted panels depicting scenes from the Bible. It was all commissioned by the Goodwin family who also provided two rectors, father and son, for 94 years from 1806 to 1900.

Other notable buildings in the village include 'Mabbutts', the oldest surviving house, which is timber-framed with overhangs and

119

was built in the very early 16th century. The watermill stands on a cut to the east of the village and straddles the boundary with Linton. The windmill, built in a field to the south of the watermill in 1837, has been developed into two houses.

During renovation of Burford House, a farmhouse previously believed to be from the late 17th century, some murals were uncovered from Cromwellian days depicting distinct Royalist tendencies by the owners. These have been restored and can be seen by written application to Burford House, Hildersham.

✹ HILTON

The parish of Hilton lies on the edge of the fens on slightly higher ground, as the name suggests. The village is surrounded by fields that are cultivated for cereal crops and the vivid yellow flowering oil-seed rape.

Old and new houses with generous gardens are set around the green and along the streets. Shady paths lead over white painted footbridges crossing the ditches that drain the land. The water collects in weed covered ponds over which ancient willows drape their branches. At one point the water crosses the road making the ford quite deep in rainy weather.

The old farmhouses such as Manor Farm, College Farm, Cross Farm and Oaktree Farm tell of the once rural occupation. The modern village has no working farms, but the land around is still farmed commercially by a small number of farming organisations.

From the 85 houses and 535 population in 1881 the village has grown to over 350 houses and over 1,000 population. People of all lifestyles reside here now. The 19th century village and surrounding area supported self sufficient life with a butcher, a baker, two general stores, a carpenter, a blacksmith and four public houses. Today only one general store, the post office and the Prince of Wales pub remain. A motor repair workshop serves the needs of modern day transport.

Many visitors are attracted by the picturesque village green with its maze dating back to 1660. It is one of only eight surviving turf mazes in England, and has recently been restored to English Heritage standards. The monument in the centre commemorates William Sparrow who created the maze.

The green is all that remains of the once extensive common land villagers used for grazing cattle. Even today, the right to pasture 15 cows is still attached to some properties. Alas, there are no cows to be seen. They have given place to the cricket ground and the football field. 'Capability' Brown, famous for his landscape gardening, may have had a hand in the layout of Hilton Green, as he was at one time lord of the manor of Fenstanton and Hilton. In spite of having lost the elms and large beeches there are still a great number of magnificent trees. The walnut trees planted in the 1950s are now mature and are enjoyed especially in autumn when the crop is ripe.

The old village school was closed in 1955 after over 100 years of use and the children travel by bus to Fenstanton. After restoration the picturesque building has found a new purpose as the village hall and is again a central feature of village life.

Standing on the highest point, surrounded by the walled graveyard and old trees, is the church of St Mary Magdalene. Although mostly dating from the 14th and 15th century, parts go back to the 12th century. There is a peal of six bells – the latest two were dedicated in December 1987. Not far from it is the Methodist church which was built in 1867.

Hilton is a friendly and welcoming place with an active community life. This is clearly evident in the many clubs and activities supported within the village, among them the celebration of Feast Week commemorating the Feast of St Mary Magdalene which falls on 22nd July.

❧ HINXTON

Hinxton is Anglo-Saxon for 'Hengest's farm', but archaeological excavations during the past decade have shown that our Neolithic ancestors (4400–2000 BC) worked in the area. There have been extensive finds of Roman and Saxon artefacts and Hinxton is recorded in the Domesday Book. The church of St Mary and St John dates from 1150. The watermill, which functioned until 1955, was restored by the Cambridge Preservation Society in 1986 and it is open on Sunday afternoon in the summer.

At the end of the First World War there were two grocery shops, a butcher's shop, a post office, dairy, two public houses, the village school, the Congregational chapel, four farms and some smallholdings. Now there is one public house and two farms. However, Hinxton is now on the world map, as far as scientific research is concerned, because The Wellcome Trust bought the Hinxton Estate in 1992. The Georgian Hinxton Hall has been lavishly restored and new buildings and landscaping provide an attractive environment for both villagers and employees. The ultra modern buildings which comprise the Sanger Centre, where the genome sequencing takes place, provide a striking contrast to other village architecture. The Red Lion dates from the 17th century, but Lordship Farm, with the remains of a moat, is believed to be much older. The Old Manor House, opposite the pub, contains interesting wall paintings, possibly Tudor. The Oak House, with its massive beams and attractive brick work, was once a farmhouse and two cottages. Church Green Cottage is another fine old building with a thatched roof – formerly four small cottages.

Changes to the village have often been caused by fire. We are told that on Tuesday 6th March 1743 a terrible fire occurred. It began at 11 am at the malting of Mr Burling, who burned his malt with straw, inadvisedly, when the wind was high. Ten houses were consumed in four hours.

Two developments of low rent homes for young village families have been built since 1990. This has helped to keep a good number of children in the community. Three retirement bungalows have been purchased by the trustees of Hinxton's Anne Howsden Charity. This charity dates from the mid 1600s and there is an annual distribution of coal, or other help with heating, to those in need.

In the past the Hinxton Feast was held on 26th June, but the Church and Village Fete in early June has taken its place and most of the population of 350 join in the fun at the village hall and playing field.

❦ HISTON & IMPINGTON

Histon and Impington, lying approximately four miles north west of Cambridge, have a population of about 7,000 and are almost one village in that the boundaries are intermingled. Each has its own Parish Council and so far all attempts to amalgamate have been unsuccessful.

Both villages are mentioned in the Domesday Book and Impington was recorded in an Anglo-Saxon charter dated AD 991. However, there is no earlier record of Histon (the larger of the two) although there is no doubt that a settlement existed in former times.

Mrs Elizabeth Woodcock of Impington has gone down in history as a result of having survived being buried in the snow for eight days in 1799. She attended Cambridge market on Saturday 2nd February and on her return she was thrown (or fell) from her horse and took shelter under a hedge. The snow drifted over her until she was completely covered. Eventually she found an aperture in the snow through which she pushed a red handkerchief tied to a stick, which led to her discovery, but not until the following Sunday!

Moses Carter, the Histon giant, was over seven feet tall and lived in the 19th century. His tall hat and one of his boots are still in existence and schoolchildren are delighted when they are allowed to try on the hat!

Each village has a 13th century parish church and there is also one Baptist church, one Methodist church and a Salvation Army hall, all with their own social activities. Spurgeon, the famous Baptist preacher, is known to have given sermons in a barn on the green.

The red brick Old House (the first brick built house in Histon) is said to be haunted and contains two priests' hiding holes. It is believed to date from the 16th century and for many years was thought to have been the oldest house. But recent discoveries indicate that the thatched Stone Corner cottage is even older and could have been a guildhall probably dating from the 14th century.

Chivers & Sons Ltd started their jam making in a barn at Impington in 1873. This grew so much that in 1875 a factory was built near Histon station with a siding for its own use and employing some 4,000 people at its peak. Messrs Chivers were extremely good employers and provided many facilities for both their own workers and the villagers; for instance in 1903 a Men's Institute was opened in the old Baptist chapel on the green which incorporated a reading room, billiards room and a gymnasium. Baths were also provided, which were quite an innovation.

Unwins Seeds Ltd is another firm which started from small beginnings and which is known throughout the country, especially for its sweetpeas which were developed by the founder of the firm, Mr W.J. Unwin. People from many parts of the country visit the trial grounds during the summer.

A beautiful stained glass window was erected in Impington church in 1991 in which can be seen apples and pears to commemorate Chivers, together with sweet peas and gladioli for Unwins. Both firms have given a great deal of support to Impington in the 20th century.

The village green, which is in Histon, has a brook running through it on which are many ducks. It is a picturesque spot which attracts many visitors, with a large grassy area, beautiful trees and a variety of interesting houses around. The village pump still stands in its original position and it is thought that at one time there were stocks nearby.

Impington Village College was opened in 1939 as a secondary school and has been greatly added to over the years, more recently by the addition of accommodation for handicapped children. Designed by the well-known architects Walter Gropius and Maxwell Fry, it also included an adult centre and was built on land given by the Chiver family which was part of Impington Hall estate. The Hall was demolished in 1953 but had at one time been occupied by Talbot Pepys who was visited there by his nephew, the diarist Samuel Pepys. The name is commemorated in one of the roads, Pepys Terrace.

Over the years both villages have grown tremendously and Vision Park, with its offices and high tech industrial tenants, has been added as well as the Post House Hotel and the private Lea Hospital.

❧ HOLME

Holme is situated on the B660 south of Peterborough, two miles east of the A1(M). Although it is a small village it has some claim to fame. Just outside the village on Holme Fen is the lowest road in England, nine to ten feet below sea level at the last measurement taken for the *Guinness Book of Records*.

During the 19th century William Wells, the squire, reclaimed the land from Whittlesey Mere by drainage. Although he unfortunately spent all the family wealth, the village is now blessed with some of the best arable land in the East of England.

In 1851 on the south west edge of Whittlesey Mere an iron post was driven into the peat, flush with the surface. To this day we are still able to measure peat shrinkage by the famous Iron Post. This post, reputedly from the Crystal Palace Exhibition, replaced wooden posts which had been driven in during 1848.

St Giles' church is relatively modern, built in the mid 19th century, but there has been a church on the site for many centuries. Behind the church is the oldest dwelling in the village, dating from 1770.

The squire's family lived in Holmewood Hall, rebuilt in 1873, which became a field station and offices for the British Sugar Corporation, who restored some of the rooms to their former glory.

There are a few farm cottages built in the Gothic style popular in the 19th century. The old vicarage, built in 1859, stands in Station Road and opposite is the post office, the corner of which is rounded to enable carts to negotiate the narrow lanes more easily.

The eastern boundary of the village is the level crossing developed when the Great Northern and LNER railways built a station (unfortunately closed in the 1960s). There was also a branch line to Ramsey and a wharf where farm produce was off loaded from horse-drawn barges, which were then reloaded with coal for the pumping engines on the fens.

❧ Holywell-cum-Needingworth

Holywell-cum-Needingworth is a village which is situated on the river Ouse about two miles from St Ives. Holywell was the name given to the area around the well in the churchyard; Needingworth developed, further inland, much later.

The church of St John the Baptist stands upon a hill and it is thought a beacon once stood there to guide navigators of skiffs and barks that travelled the black waters of the fens. Each June there is a well-dressing and the church is decorated for the Church Festival.

Holywell is a defended village – the houses are built in a circle facing outwards – and this is still clear today. It is also raised as the river floods the meadows alongside regularly. Many of the houses were built by Dutch settlers in the 17th century who came to help drain the land and make it suitable for farming. There are still many old houses in Holywell, especially the Ferryboat Inn, which is in the *Guinness Book of Records* as the oldest inn in England and is reputed to be haunted. The Pike and Eel is another old hostelry by the river, about a mile from the

126

main village, where there used to be a chain ferry to Over.

Most of the old houses in Needingworth were destroyed in the fire of 1847. A pair of fire-hooks, used for pulling down burning thatch, can be seen hanging on a brick wall in the High Street. Needingworth has been much developed and is now the main part of the parish. It has an old lock-up, dating from 1838; this stands next to the war memorial.

The village has recently been bypassed and this makes it quieter, cleaner and safer. In the spring the daffodils at each end are a welcoming sight.

☙ HOUGHTON & WYTON

Houghton and Wyton, adjoining picturesque villages, are situated midway between St Ives and Huntingdon on the north bank of the winding Great Ouse river. Famed for their natural rural beauty the villages offer an interesting mix of thatched and whitewashed cottages, imposing Georgian residences redolent with history and ghosts, sturdy dwellings once owned by yeoman farmers and modern brick-built houses and bungalows, in all about 700 homes.

The most well-known landmark is the timber and brick watermill which has been a National Trust property for many years and attracts large numbers of visitors. A mill has stood by the river there for over a thousand years.

Facing the green and the centre of Houghton is the oldest house in the villages. Built in the 15th century it was once a public house called the George and Dragon but it is now privately owned. A thatched clock tower occupies a central point on the green which has the three village shops clustered around it. The marble bust of Potto Brown, the noted local philanthropist, gazes sternly over the green. He built the chapel and a school and ran the mill during the 19th century.

As well as the three shops the villages share a church, two flourishing pubs, a garage and a post office.

127

The typical occupations of the residents have changed with the years. Previously mainly agricultural, many jobs now involve commuting to London or Cambridge. Many service and civilian personnel from Wyton RAF base also live in the villages.

During the summer Houghton Lock is busy with cruisers and narrow boats. Punts and rowing boats can be hired nearby. The river attracts walkers, ornithologists and anglers all year round.

🍁 ICKLETON

Ickleton, a village with a population of 500, lies on the west bank of the river Cam near the southern border of Cambridgeshire.

The village was mentioned in the Domesday survey and its history is recorded on an admirable series of hassocks in St Mary Magdalene's church, Ickleton's most important historic building, which has a working peal of eight bells.

The hassocks show the Roman occupation of Ickleton in AD 43 and carry the story through the Saxons to the Conqueror, through battles, plague and religious intolerance to the arson fire of 1979 which destroyed the chancel roof, the organ and the medieval painted ceiling under the bell tower. But, perhaps as compensation, the cleaning process after the fire revealed a rare 12th century mural of the Last Supper and events leading up to the Crucifixion and a later Doom painting, which attract many art historians to the church.

Sheep were an all important part of village life and a hundred years ago there were two fulling mills where wool was carded and felted, giving employment to many and leaving a memorial in the family name of Carder, extant in the village today. At that time Ickleton was self sufficient, having three butchers, two bakers, two dairies, two tailors, three grocers, a clockmaker and two weavers. A local family ran the blacksmiths yard which contained not only five forges manned by eight blacksmith's, but also a paint shop, an ironmonger, a wheelwright's shop and sheds on legs for the seasoning of timber and coffin boards.

An undulation in a field in Top Town marks the position of the saw-pit where travelling sawyers worked long hours of hard skilled labour. After 14 working days they would 'go on the drink' for seven, frequenting the six public houses then open in the village, which were run by the landlords' wives. Women and children always worked in the fields, and to a lesser degree still do, potato picking, gathering root crops and pulling wild oats from the growing wheat and barley.

But it was not all work for the people of Ickleton. A charter for a weekly market was granted in 1227, and for 600 years an annual fair was held on 22nd July. This was only discontinued in 1875. Down the years there have been ox roastings, harvest homes, bonfire nights and the ever popular May Day celebrations which gave the children a holiday. The girls would gather paigles (cowslips) and daisies for garlands and dance round the maypole, singing:

> The 1st of May is Garland Day,
> Please, I bring my Garland.
> The 1st and 2nd and 3rd of May
> Are Chimney Sweep and Garland Day.

The village school has become the village hall and children attend schools in Duxford, Sawston and Cambridge. Today, tractors have replaced working horses and far less manual labour is required on the farms. Men and women find work outside the village, which sometimes seems entirely deserted during the day, though a few light industries have recently sprung up in the village itself. The noise of traffic from the M11 motorway has taken over the from the sound of hammer on anvil and the bustle of people and farm animals passing to and fro in the streets. The many ancient charities existing since 1558 were combined in 1980, still serving the inhabitants in many ways.

🍁 ISLEHAM

Isleham is a very old place of habitation. There is evidence that people have been living here since prehistoric times and Western Europe's largest hoard of bronze artefacts was found here in 1960. Until 1939 there were no paved roads to the west (Soham) or north (Prickwillow and Ely) and reliance was on one poor road in and out and mainly on green highways (droves) or waterways, though a railway came and went in the span of one man's life. As a result the inhabitants were self sufficient, great traders by water, fiercely independent and possessed of great skills and hidden abilities, which provided their strength and tenacity.

This independent spirit, and support for Oliver Cromwell in the Civil War, led to the departure to America of the Bernard/Peyton family (who had been lords of the manor since medieval times) at the Restoration of Charles II. Only recently a member of the family, Charles Peyton, again became lord of the manor, but he does not live here.

Charming (many listed) buildings include the 9th century priory church of St Margaret, the beautiful 14th century church of St Andrew with 15th century brasses and a hammerbeam 'angel' roof, a Tudor warehouse, many Elizabethan houses, and almshouses founded by Lady Frances Peyton in 1582 and still run by the trustees.

The Independent chapel in Pound Lane is one of the earliest 'free' chapels in the country, and it was to this chapel that the famous evangelist the Rev Spurgeon came as a young man, from Newmarket, to be baptised at Isleham Ferry in the river Lark on 3rd May 1850. Today there are a church and two chapels, all well supported with active Sunday schools.

Mature trees are plentiful, new ones are planted yearly and the parish recreation ground is well used for sports and other functions – the cricket team reached the national village champion's finals at Lords in 1975. The football teams do well and have produced at least three county referees and were playing on winter evenings by floodlight at least thirty years ago! There is a good modern village hall, much used.

The 'Fifties Charity' founded in 1477 for the benefit of the poor, in 1848 paid for the salary of the schoolmaster at the first school in the village and still supplies many extras to the Isleham primary school. It also supports educational projects for those under 25, as well as 'dole' vouchers to purchase food at Christmas for all retired villagers, regardless of need – recipients can always give equivalent money to those less fortunate.

There is now an Isleham Society which has regular lectures on many subjects. It attracts newcomers to the village who have taken up residence in the many new houses and bungalows built in recent years.

🍁 KEYSTON

Keyston stands on the B663, which runs from the A14 on the western edge of Cambridgeshire through to Raunds in Northamptonshire. The name should rightly be spelt Keystone, meaning Ketil's Stone, probably a boundary marker of the western-most limit of the shire, some 1,100 or more years ago.

Keyston at the time of the Domesday Book belonged to the King and had some 32 villagers. Nowadays the population is approximately 130. Farming still provides significant employment and the village inn – formerly known as the White Horse – is now famous locally as the Pheasant.

The village hall was recently converted from an old stone threshing barn and is widely used, with excellent facilities.

The church is a distinguished building standing in the centre of the village, dating back to the 15th century. It is aisled with transepts. The western entrance is recessed into the tower to form a very elaborate doorway and porch combined. The lectern is 17th century and there is medieval glass in the window tracery.

Opposite Manor Farm House, running up towards the church, is a beautifully landscaped water garden, constructed about 1960 for the enjoyment of an elderly lady living in the Manor House at the time.

🍁 KIMBOLTON

Kimbolton is set in the gently undulating, partly wooded, agricultural countryside of south west Cambridgeshire, with Bedfordshire and Northamptonshire as close neighbours. This part of the county was originally Huntingdonshire.

The river Kym runs along the north eastern fringe. There is a wide main street, with buildings that are typically medieval and timber-framed but with Georgian façades. At one end of the street is the castle and at the other the church of St Andrew, mentioned in the Domesday Book, promoted from timber to stone around 1200, with a number of significant additions and alterations until the Reformation. Limited archaeological finds within the parish suggest there were Roman settlers, and the indications are that Kimbolton was capital of the Leightonstone Hundred well before the Norman invasion and may have become 'nucleated' earlier than most settlements in this area. At Domesday the population was between 500 and 600, second only in Huntingdonshire to the county town itself. The present layout is probably the result of the market charter granted in 1200 by King John to the Lord of the manor, Geoffrey Fitzpiers, who was his Chief Justiciar. From this period date Newtown and the diversions of the main road through the Market Place, hence the notorious bends. East Street, running parallel with the High Street market, acted as a service street.

Kimbolton centre and the castle grounds have been designated a Conservation Area of outstanding merit.

The main tourist attraction is Kimbolton Castle, where Catherine of Aragon died in 1536. It has a medieval core but the conversion by

Vanbrugh in the early 1700s is the most apparent feature today. For much of its early history it was owned by the Stafford, then the Wingfield families. In 1615 it was acquired by the Montagu family, subsequently given the titles of Dukes of Manchester. In 1950 the 10th Duke sold the building and the immediate grounds to Kimbolton School, originally a Tudor grammar school. The Castle Gatehouse, the work of Robert Adam in the 1760s, dominates the east end of the High Street. The staterooms and extensive grounds are open to the public on Spring and Late Summer Bank Holidays and on some Sunday afternoons in July and August.

Recently housing estates have been erected, mostly in Newtown, and the extra population has given a welcome fillip to the town centre shops. Geoffrey Fitzpiers' intention to bring trade to Kimbolton is still being fulfilled.

🍁 KIRTLING & UPEND

Shown in the Cambridgeshire structure plan as an 'area of outstanding beauty', Kirtling, with the adjoining hamlet of Upend, has a long history dating back to Saxon times. After many unsettled years when the Danes raided the area and several famines occurred, Kirtling estate was given by Earl Godwin to Earl Harold, later King of England. Following the Norman Conquest, William I gave the manor to his niece Countess Judith. Several generations passed until the estate was eventually purchased by Sir Edward North in about 1530, and remained with his descendants, until in the 1930s it was bought by the 1st Lord Fairhaven.

The Hall was demolished in 1801, only the Elizabethan gatehouse remaining to this day, to which a house was attached in Victorian times.

The church of All Saints is nearby with parts dating from Norman times. It has a fine doorway with a tympanum of Our Lord in Majesty, a unique collection of hatchments and a number of interesting tombs, the most outstanding of which is that erected to Roger 2nd Baron North in a chapel built to contain it. A comprehensive guide and village history booklet is available at the church.

Most of the residential part of the village lies some distance from the church. It is said that the original village which lay east of the church was abandoned after the Black Death and rebuilt further away. During this century many cottages have been demolished, as the only industry, farming, has become mechanised requiring fewer employees, and this now gives the village a scattered appearance. Nevertheless it is a 'live' village with several generations of older families still living fairly close to each other.

There are a number of listed buildings and numerous thatched cottages which have been pleasingly restored. The small amount of modern development has been thoughtfully undertaken and blends in well with the older property. There is a most attractive village sign depicting a Saxon and his dog, and a well-maintained village hall.

With a population of approximately 300, the village has two public houses, the Queen's Head and the Red Lion, both thriving. There is a very successful Cricket Club with a superbly kept pitch and on the first Saturday in September each year a magnificent show of produce and handicrafts.

The village has a post office and shop combined, a new village hall, a garage (repairs only), stud farms equipped with the most modern facilities for horses, several large farms and some smallholdings. The water piped from Denver Sluice in Norfolk, destined for use in Essex, is brought to the surface in Kirtling and descends many 'steps' until it reaches the river Stour which rises in the vicinity.

Upend is now designated a 'conservation village' and is a beauty spot in spring. It boasts one of the very few listed red telephone kiosks! The churchyard is also a delight in spring when carpeted with snowdrops and at its gate is a VR post box set into the wall.

🍁 LANDBEACH

The name Landbeach is derived from medieval times when sheep were brought here from nearby Waterbeach when the pastures there were flooded. It is still a fairly small village with just over 250 dwellings.

It is worth diverting from the Cambridge to Ely road to come to Landbeach. If the wishes of the rector, Robert Masters, and the villagers had been granted in 1763 this main road would have been built through the village, but the 'powers that be' at that time decided to ignore the village road and repair the highway, which is now the A10. This decision upset the villagers particularly as they were required 'to do statute work thereon for a certain number of days'. It was most fortunate though as far as the present day inhabitants are concerned for although heavy traffic is only half a mile away it is hardly audible. The village is quiet and peaceful, a haven for those living here.

The Baptist chapel is on the left going in the direction of Ely. It is a handsome building, erected in 1854. It was frequently visited by the famous preacher Charles Haddon Spurgeon. If the congregation was too large to fit into the chapel, he would stand on a cattle crib and preach in the field opposite.

The High Street curves through the village giving a pleasant scene each time a corner is turned. The road is bordered by a mixture of dwellings, Victorian, medieval and modern, which blend in well and present a pleasant variety. Beyond the houses on either side is farmland which produces most arable crops.

The Plague House is a thatched cottage on the corner of Abraham's Close, so called since 1665 when two ladies lived here to escape the great plague of London. The only person to assist them was the rector who unfortunately passed the illness to his family and servants who succumbed to the disease. The rector himself died a year later. This fact has not detracted from its desirability as a dwelling; it

Landbeach Tithe Barn

continues to be well maintained and enhances the High Street.

Landbeach possesses a tithe barn which has been preserved for posterity. The black timbered frame and massive thatched roof possess an air of permanence even though the surrounding countryside has changed. It was built over 400 years ago when a canal ran through the village and barge traffic was common. It is reached by a footpath and the interior may be viewed, the key being obtainable from the village shop.

The parish church of All Saints is a fine example of medieval architecture and the spire acts as a landmark as it is visible for miles around. Matthew Parker (nosey Parker) is the most famous Landbeach resident. He became rector at the time of great upheaval with the Christian Church, the Reformation. He was subsequently appointed Archbishop of Canterbury by Queen Elizabeth I.

There have been a number of changes within the village in recent years. There is no longer a post office or village store, but there is one shop, the owner of which provides an invaluable service to the village. A pocket park now exists on former farmland and a circular walk through newly planted woods gives excellent views of nearby farms and villages.

The village sign which stands at the crossroads encapsulates the Landbeach scene by showing the church, a thatched cottage, sheep, the tithe barn and the golden mitre of Archbishop Matthew Parker.

LEVERINGTON

Leverington is situated two miles north of Wisbech. It has a population of 4,500–5,000 but this is increasing every day because of the development of several private housing estates. The village has many amenities for its occupants which include one church, two pubs, one general store, a post office, butcher's shop, hairdresser and fish shop. There are also several small industries in the village, with seven council-owned mini factories, three engineering workshops, three garages and Colemans' bus station. However, the main occupation of the village is fruit, flower and agricultural farming.

In the centre of Leverington stands St Leonard's church, parts of which were built in the 13th century, and it was added to in the 14th and 15th centuries. It stands out as a landmark as it has a beautiful tall steeple set into a Norman turret, with four smaller turrets to support it. The church has a large congregation and during the festive season there is standing room only.

The county primary school is opposite the church and has over 185 pupils. On the site where the school stands today, there used to be a town hall, and 100 years ago there were three schools in the village, a church school and two others. These three schools were run with financial assistance from the Feoffees Charity. This charity still exists today, but its earliest deed is dated 9th October 1634, and this refers to an earlier deed dated 20th January 1555. The general practice had been for the lands to be administered by twelve feoffees, and when six died the survivors were to appoint six additional ones. Money today is issued once a year to the old and widowed of the parish and education grants are given to the school and to students for scholarships.

The village hall is the centre where many organisations meet. The village also has a large sports field where football and cricket are played regularly. The ground was left to the village people by the Munday family and its upkeep is supervised by a Sports Field Committee. The elderly are also catered for in the village by Roman Court, a warden controlled complex.

Leverington Hall was never a manor house. It was built by the Swaine family in the 17th century. It has a long and somewhat colourful history. At one point the family who owned it were so numerous that the kitchen cooper was used for preparing the family's meals, as the ordinary domestic appliances were woefully inadequate.

Park House is a lovely old house but its exact age is not known. The rear has Tudor characteristics with a Georgian façade. It is beautifully preserved and much of it is in its original state. It is surrounded by parkland with many magnificent trees still standing. The Lumpkin family were owners for many years and strong rumour says that Oliver Goldsmith wrote *She Stoops to Conquer* whilst staying at Park House.

🍁 LINTON

Iron Age people and later the Romans settled here, but it was the Saxons who not only left a burial ground but also, in AD 725 specifically recorded the place as 'the farmstead in the flaxfields' and so gave Linton its name. The blue of flax which doubtless adorned the area over many centuries was last seen at the farm of Little Linton during and after the Second World War when there were renewed demands for its fibres. To the outsider, this south eastern corner of the county, where the East Anglian Heights provide hilly but open countryside, looks predominantly rural, and it was only when the 20th century was well advanced that agriculture ceased to be the main occupation.

The river Granta encouraged settlement and by the Middle Ages there was a thriving market town. Its early importance is revealed in the Conservation Area which consists of the long, narrow High Street, once the main road to Colchester but now bypassed, and a number of adjacent lanes. Here you will find low thatched cottages, jettied timber-framed buildings, brick façades, the occasional mansard roof and walls in a succession of white and pastel shades, the pinks reminiscent of bygone days when juice from the ubiquitous sloe was used as colouring for exterior plasterwork.

For a walk within the Conservation Area turn off the High Street into Church Lane flanked by characteristic high flint walls, take a look at the impressive jettied timber framed guildhall dating from the early 1500s and turn into the churchyard shaded by ancient yew trees. The parish church of St Mary the Virgin is a flint faced building which still holds vestiges of its Norman past but is outwardly predominantly Perpendicular. The interior was dramatically refurbished just over 100 years ago when galleries, box pews and a three decker pulpit were removed to produce the spaciousness of today.

Continue the walk by crossing the footbridge over the river and once in Horn Lane come to the United Reformed church. Dissent was strong in the 1600s and after the Act of Toleration in 1689 dissenters met openly first in a barn and later in a more permanent building which was followed by the present church built in 1818. The graveyard is noteworthy. A broad path leading up to the church is flanked by massive chest tombs under which lie family burial chambers. Together they form a rare and impressive collection, the subject of a preservation order.

'Chandlers' in the High Street, thought to date from the 14th century, is probably the oldest domestic building in the village. On one of its outside walls rests a heavy iron fire-hook with a 20 ft handle, a reminder of the threat from fire in days when the majority of roofs were thatched. It was used to tear down burning thatch and prevent fire spreading, but must have been an unwieldy thing to handle even when supported on a trolley.

Known sometimes as The Pepperpot, the water tower stands atop Rivey Hill, one of the highest points in the county at just under 370 ft. The tower, Gothic in style with its pierced dark brick walls and slate capped roof, was completed in the mid 1930s, bringing to the village its first piped water. At about the same time another wonder, public electricity, came and both services must have revolutionised domestic life. New building increased and in due time new estates sprang up on the flanks of the old nucleus.

On the south west slopes of Rivey Hill lie the vineyards of Chilford Hundred Wine Company which perpetuates the name by which the area was known in feudal times. Vines of hardy German stock produce white wines made and bottled on the premises. Orders have come not only from this country but from France and as far afield as Japan.

The population of Linton is 4,010 and the children benefit from three schools, Infant, Junior and the academically excellent Village College, which serves ten other villages. There are two industrial areas which provide employment.

The Zoological Gardens situated on Hadstock Road provide a happy outing for families from a wide area and the lions can be heard roaring in the night.

🍁 LITLINGTON

The village of Litlington nestles between The Mordens and Bassingbourn in south west Cambridgeshire. In the 1960s it was described as somewhat 'higgledy-piggledy' but since those days building of new houses has taken place and there is a mixture of old and new dwellings blending together. All the same the village has tangible evidence of its great age. Extensive Roman remains were unearthed in 1912 at Manor Farm – a villa with hot and cold baths, urns full of ashes and various pots and vessels. Earlier in 1821 some men digging in a field called 'Heaven's Walls' discovered what proved to have been a Roman burial ground.

The parish church of St Catherine is in the patronage of Clare College. Of local clunch and flint construction, it has a nave of the Decorated period (circa 1270) and 13th and 14th century aisles. The lower part of the tower is Early English (circa 1170) and the upper part is of the Decorated period, as is the chancel. The registers date from 1599 and the list of vicars from 1313. The church plate includes a chalice and cover of 1676/7 date.

When the Americans of the 355th Fighter Group took over from the RAF the Steeple Mordern airfield, Litlington was inundated with hutments and temporary buildings, some of which were later used in the village. In the meantime villagers made many friends among Americans and are still remembered today. The large military lorries

The Cage, Litlington

141

thundering through the village led to a one-way system – the order was rescinded after the war but brought back into being in the 1970s – this must surely be one of the few villages, if not the only one, with such a traffic system. On their return visits over the years since the Second World War, the Americans often refer to the tower of St Catherine's, as during those war days many young airmen were heard to say on returning from a mission over enemy territory 'when we see the tower of St Catherine's we know we are safely home'. In May 1993 a beautiful stained glass window in memory of the 355th Fighter Group was dedicated. It was made by Mr John Dobbentin who lives in Woodstock, about an hour's journey from Chicago, and was flown over from the United States.

One of the buildings not far from the Congregational church was used as a temporary village hall after the Americans returned home, until the present one was built in the 1970s. Another such building, used by the Americans as a chapel and gymnasium in Abington Piggotts Road, was reconstructed to provide a temporary school when the children moved from the Victorian building next to the church, although this school continued to be used for children from Bassingbourn for woodwork classes before the Bassingbourn Village College was built. It had also been used by an engineering firm.

In 1982 the Litlington primary school was closed and the children bussed to Steeple Morden. Many villagers thought at the time that the heart had gone out of the village and parents fought hard for a new school.

Whether or not a Litlington man sailed round the world with Sir Francis Drake, as legend suggests, is not quite clear. But on the mullion of a window in the south aisle of the church is an inscription in Latin – 'Francis Drake about to start on his voyage, 1595' – by the Lord of the Manor of Huntingfield. On the opposite side of the church a pillar bears the inscription 'as on sea so on land' – by Sherman's bailiff, Robert Bolnest. It would certainly appear that there was some link.

Litlington's population rose from around 350 in 1801 to 796 during the 'coprolite era', like other villages in this corner of the county. At that time there were a good number of public houses in the village – in 1960 they were down to three, the Royal Oak, the Crown and the Beehive. Today there is one, the Crown, to serve the present population of some 820.

One relic of ancient history still stands on a remaining portion of the green known as St Peter's Hill. This is a lock-up, known locally as The Cage – not many of these solid solitary cells remain. It is recorded that the last man put in The Cage in 1840 set fire to the truss of straw provided for him. Further to the south is a large triangular portion of the green. It was here and in the adjoining Seven Stars meadow that fairs were held until the late 1950s.

🍁 LITTLE PAXTON

Little Paxton is situated near St Neots, just off the A1. It has developed from an early Stone Age settlement, to being part of the estates of Riversfield, Paxton Hall and Paxton Park.

The development of the park and estates for modern housing and the gravel extraction area has again transformed the locality.

Not only is the village near major road and rail routes but it also has the Great Ouse, a navigable river, as one boundary. One of its most popular recreational facilities is the Paxton Pits Nature Reserve, which offers opportunities for walking, sailing, bird watching and fishing, with various activities organised by the RSPB and the Friends of Paxton Pits Nature Reserve.

🍁 LITTLEPORT

Everyone in the fens knows Littleport, they had riots there didn't they? Yes, as far back as the 13th century the people had rioted against the threatened drainage of the fen when they thought that their livelihood was threatened, but the Littleport Riot of 1816 was an entirely different thing. Farm workers and men returning home from the Napoleonic wars faced unemployment and starvation, and parish relief was scarcely enough to keep body and soul together. The callousness of the Parish Officer eventually goaded the men and they rioted from Littleport to Ely before the military were called in to round them up. Twenty-four, including one woman, were sentenced to be hanged. Later 19 of them were reprieved and transported to Botany Bay.

There was great local sympathy for the rioters, and both the builder who had supplied the cart to take the five condemned to the gallows and the carpenter who made the coffins soon met their deaths in mysterious circumstances. The five hanged rioters were buried in one grave at Ely, and there is a memorial tablet in the tower of St Mary's church to remind people of the riots. It is interesting to note that the Transport and General Workers Union maintained a rest home at Littleport until quite recently; as good a memorial to the five dead men as they could perhaps have wished.

Legend has it that King Canute founded this fishing village on the Ouse and named it Littleport. Until recently it provided dock and warehouse facilities serving barges from Kings Lynn. Now the cargo port has given way to a modern marina to service the river pleasure boat trade.

Littleport lies five miles north of Ely on the A10, and is set to expand since the bypass diverted the heavy traffic and at the same time cut the travel time from Cambridge. Population has slowly grown over the past century from 4,157 in 1891 to 5,840 in 1986. Village industry is still largely based on agriculture – packing and transporting vegetables grown on the surrounding fens, but the largest employer has a world famous name, Burberry's Clothing. Burberry's own the 'shirt factory' as it is still called, an industry set up by a Mr Thomas Peacock in 1881 to provide work for the village women during the agricultural depression. He called his company Hope Brothers, wanting to give the villagers something to hope for, and in less than ten years it was employing 400 workers.

At the turn of the century Littleport was the mecca of ice skating. The moors, close by the railway station, were flooded in winter to provide the finest skating facilities in England. Excursions were run from Liverpool Street, and amid music and bright lighting the skaters raced for prizes ranging from a pig for the local ladies to the Grand Silver Challenge Cup worth 50 guineas and competed for by the world's greatest speed men.

Today, Littleport's big summer attraction is 'the show'. The largest in the Isle of Ely area, it is The East Cambridgeshire Show in all but name. The show is the successor of the old Littleport Feast which took place over three days every July, culminating in water sports when it is said there was *always* a thunderstorm! The sports traditionally ended with a water polo match and then diving from the top of Sandhill Bridge, but the show is firmly land-based these days!

🍁 LITTLE THETFORD

Little Thetford is a small village two miles from Ely off the A10. It is possible that it dates back to the Bronze Age as a bronze sickle, rings and pottery have been found in the area. Years ago, the monks of Ely used to come to the river and fish for eels, and in the early days of the 20th century there was a windmill beside the river with a floatbridge manned by the wife of the miller.

The oldest building in the village is St George's church of 14th century origin, consisting of a nave, chancel, north porch and south vestry, with beautiful stained glass windows behind the altar.

In the early days the Baptists worshipped in the open air, later using the clubroom of the Wheatsheaf public house for their meetings, until the existing chapel was built in 1867.

At one time, there were five public houses in the village. The Wheatsheaf later became the post office and shop, now closed, while the Three Horseshoes and April Thatch became private houses. On the road between Stretham and Ely were two others, one named

Quarterway House, the other the Halfway House, also now privately owned dwellings. All the public houses were no doubt justified as many people worked on the land, and looked forward to pleasant evenings drinking with their friends.

The village pond, long since gone, was opposite the Three Horseshoes. There were always ducks swimming around, and it was also used by farmers who would walk their horses through it after working on the fields.

The village school was built in 1871 – prior to that pupils were taught in a hired room lent by the Townsend Charity. One elderly resident recalls paying one penny per week for her education. The school was modernised in 1959 and a special service was held in the church to mark the occasion.

Originally thatched houses and cottages were situated in the main street, but the only thatched houses left standing are Horseshoes, April Thatch and the Round House. The latter, formerly a dovecote, was later converted into two dwellings, until some years ago it was restored to the charming and unique house which it is today. Many of the old cottages and houses have been demolished and replaced by modern houses and bungalows, and all the residents take pride in their gardens.

The old manor house, formerly occupied by farming families, became derelict in the 1970s and was replaced by a row of modern houses.

The house opposite the church known as Church Farm has an interesting history. In 1945 it was a two storey building until the thatched roof caught fire and the top storey was burnt out. A previous resident has recalled that for many years an elderly lady – a churchwarden – had resided there, and after her death strange tapping noises were heard on the long landing. She had walked with a stick, so these noises were attributed to her. After the fire in the house, no more tapping was heard.

❧ LITTLE WILBRAHAM

Little Wilbraham is a small village, probably best described as a hamlet, which is situated about seven miles from Cambridge, six miles from Newmarket and one mile from its big sister village, Great Wilbraham.

The origins of the village go back to Saxon times, but hardly any evidence of antiquity now remains except for the 12th century church and one or two timber-framed Tudor houses and a windmill now, alas, no longer working, but redesigned as an interesting home.

Once there was a butcher's shop on part of Manor Farm which was a thriving business until one day the butcher's indelible pencil accidentally fell into the sausage machine resulting in purple sausages! After this business unaccountably declined!

To the west of the village is Wilbraham Fen, an area of rough and boggy land, but of great botanical interest because of a profusion of wild flowers, peculiar to fenland, which includes Purple Loosestrife, Meadow Rue, Tufted Hair Grass, Harebell and Field Scabious.

There is no through road in the village which now consists of privately owned and council property. There is also the Hole in the Wall, a 15th century public house and restaurant so named because of the hole in the wall of the building where the farm workers used to come and have their flasks and jugs filled.

It is a pleasant country village whose main purpose is to serve as a dormitory for those of its residents who work in Cambridge, Newmarket and surrounding farms.

❧ LODE WITH LONGMEADOW

Off the busy B1102, and almost halfway between Cambridge and Newmarket, is the village of Lode and its hamlet of Longmeadow. Lode has two unusual features: firstly the road through the village goes nowhere but fades into the fenland, and secondly it did not receive its own identity until 1894 when a Local Government Board issued an order separating it from Bottisham and it was formed into a civil parish.

Nevertheless, Lode has existed since the early 13th century, the name meaning a watercourse, the same waterway, probably of Roman origin, on which boats brought up goods to the port of Lode from the Cam, from where they were transported overland to Bottisham.

There existed also the Priory of Anglesey, founded in the reign of Henry I, for canons of the Augustinian Order, and at the time of the Dissolution of the Monasteries some 11 canons were in residence. The property fell into disrepair and passed into many hands including those of Thomas Hobson (1544–1631), the carrier who refused to allow any horse to be taken from his stables in Cambridge except in its proper turn, giving birth to the saying 'Hobson's Choice'; and Sir George Downing, the founder of Downing College in Cambridge. In 1861 the Rev John Hailstone acquired the property. Hailstone, formerly the vicar of Bottisham, did much good work in Lode. He was responsible for Lode having its own church (1853) and for the building of a school (1865).

In 1926 the Abbey was bought by the first Lord Fairhaven who transformed the then 2 acres of garden and parkland into the finest landscaped garden in the country, the new winter walk completing the present 98 acres of gardens. A unique statuary collection enhances the grounds and the house contains countless art treasures, all now administered by the National Trust.

With an area of some 2,500 acres, consisting mainly of good farming land around the village, it is no wonder that most local people, certainly before the First World War and for a few years after, were employed as landworkers or smallholders. The chief crops were oats, barley, wheat, potatoes and during the Second World War and after, sugar beet became a popular crop. A familiar sight of a field of sugar beet being 'singled' or 'chopped out' by an army of workers still remains in the minds of villagers. A small cement works flourished for a time. The National Trust is now the largest employer of local people and, as befits the times, many villagers commute to occupations that are as myriad as the imagination allows.

A strange character was William Pugh, who became vicar of Bottisham in 1811. Although he was not a Lode man, the people of Lode and Longmeadow benefit from his generosity from the proceeds of a charity that bears his name. He was a man of eccentric ways and of slovenly dress. As a Fellow of Trinity College he caused some concern by keeping to his rooms for days on end and it was said that he wore his linen until the smell became unbearable! He would then wrap it up in newspaper, carry it to the river Cam and drop it in from Trinity Bridge.

St James' church is now in a benefice with Bottisham and Stow-cum-Quay parishes. Lode also has an Independent chapel serving the surrounding villages.

The school is sadly closed to pupils and is now a teachers' centre. The grounds of the school, known as the Broughton Hall, the Fairhaven family name, will soon be home to an arboretum to be used for educating young children in appreciation and management of trees, under the direction of 'Trees for People Education Trust'. All public houses have now closed and the only licensed premises is the Lode and District Social Club. Lode can boast a full time post office and small shop, but all other shops have closed.

Sport is an integral part of village life and the tussle between Lode and Bottisham on the cricket field has over the years been well documented. Football is strongly supported and enthusiastically played as is tennis, and coarse fishing in nearby waters is a favourite sport. The surrounding fenland lends itself to many varied walks popular with both villagers and ramblers.

Longstanton

Longstanton, seven miles north west of Cambridge, was mentioned in the Domesday Book. Its old name meant 'long stone settlement'. Now three miles long, it was originally two separate villages, All Saints' and St Michael's. The church of All Saints' is in use, but St Michael's has become redundant.

The village's most famous family were the Hattons. Sir Thomas Hatton was the cousin of Sir Christopher, Chancellor to Queen Elizabeth I. Hattons lived here in a manor house now gone, until the line died out in 1812. However, the family left their mark – All Saints' church holds all the family tombs and memorials, including a fine chest tomb of the 17th century, with the recumbent figures of Sir Thomas and his wife Mary with their six children. The family crest includes a golden hind and this emblem caused Sir Francis Drake to rename his ship to honour Sir Christopher, his patron. Longstanton Women's Institute used the Golden Hind emblem on the village sign which they planned and funded in 1982.

Longstanton still retains some interesting old houses and cottages, including some with thatch, and St Michael's area still has some small meadows, old barns and an ancient pond. All Saints' church crossroads is a pretty rural area with plenty of mature trees. There are still two pumps, one in the High Street built on a platform to allow the carters access and a small domestic pump in Mills Lane. There are no longer any windmills, but a set of millstones has been retained, cleverly used as a paved entrance to St Michael's churchyard.

St Michael's church, churchyard and surrounding area are perhaps the most interesting part of the village. This small attractive church is thatched, one of only two in Cambridgeshire, and it stands in a neat churchyard with a large chestnut tree just inside its gate. Under the tree there is a canopied well with steps leading down to the water. This was a holy baptism well, thought to be very old. In 1986

Pump, High St.

The High Street pump, Longstanton

151

the villagers restored it and replaced its railings.

The village contains a mixture of housing – three groups of Army houses, because this is the home to Oakington Barracks (which is in Longstanton, not Oakington!), an area of council housing which includes attractive bungalows for the elderly, with resident warden, and new houses and bungalows, privately owned, set out in pleasant closes or built behind existing hedges or tree cover and blended in with the old. One road has a nicely landscaped pond and resident ducks.

The village is surrounded by agricultural land growing wheat, oil-seed rape, corn on the cob etc and there are numerous small-holdings. There are still a few farms with a little livestock. The area was known for its fruit growing but the closure of the railway line meant that growers no longer had a convenient way to send their produce to market. Many smallholders put out roadside stalls selling vegetables, fruit and flowers.

There have been Longstanton witches in the past. The most famous story concerns a Quaker woman, accused by a young woman, Mary Pryor, of having turned her into a bay mare and ridden her all the way to Madingley Hall! Fortunately for the Quaker woman, Mary's story was not believed by the judge at the trial. Even in Victorian times there was a well-known local witch with strange powers.

🍁 LONGTHORPE

Longthorpe is a small but recently expanded village situated about two miles west of the centre of Peterborough. The village sign under a spreading chestnut tree was put up by the WI in 1994. The village dates back to Roman times when it had a strong Roman garrison with a large fortress housing a vast brigade of legionaries and auxiliaries on the site where Thorpe Wood golf course is now situated.

The Tower, which was commissioned by William de Thorpe, is

situated almost at the centre of the present village. It has 6 foot thick walls and was originally three storeys high. One of the interesting features of the Tower is the wall paintings on the interior which were only discovered after the Second World War. They depict the seven ages of man, the five senses, kings and queens and many birds and animals common to the fens of which, of course, Peterborough is at the heart.

St Botolph's church, thought to be Saxon, was once a chapel of ease, and its original site was at the junction of Westwood Park Road and Thorpe Road. It was rebuilt at Longthorpe on its present site in 1263. The church itself boasts a magnificent bishop's chair and has an interesting leper's window.

Thorpe Hall was built between 1653 and 1656, being commissioned for the Lord Chief Justice, Oliver St John. It passed to Lord Fitzwilliam in 1793. (Originally much of Longthorpe and the surrounding area belonged to, or formed part of, the Fitzwilliam estate.) After Thorpe Hall ceased to be a family residence it was unused for many years, the last long-term use being a convalescent home run by the local health authority. It is now a hospice run by the Sue Ryder charity.

The Hall originally boasted a beautiful panelled library but this was removed some years ago and is now restored in its original form in Leeds Castle, Kent.

Holywell at Longthorpe was the termination of the track known as Abbots Walk which led from the Abbey (prior to the present cathedral).

In the present day Longthorpe is proud of its executive housing whilst retaining old world charm and character with its thatched post office and cottages. The past few years have seen office developments and Thorpe Wood police station on the outskirts of the village.

🍁 MADINGLEY

Madingley is an attractive village set amidst farm and woodland about four miles from Cambridge. There is a population of approximately 180 people. The village boasts an Elizabethan hall which was begun in the early 16th century by John Hinde, who died in 1550. His son, Sir Francis Hinde, completed the building, but in order to achieve this he pulled down and used some of the materials from St Etheldreda's church at Histon. The oak hammer beam can be seen in the roof structures of the hall. It is said that the ghost of Madingley Hall is the distressed Lady Ursula Hinde, mother of Sir Francis.

In 1948 the University of Cambridge bought the land and dwellings (then some 1,200 acres). The hall itself is now used by the Board of Extra Mural Studies, being self sufficient with lecture and residential facilities.

The present church of Mary Magdalene dates from 1092. It has a 13th century nave and 15th century porch. The Norman font to be seen in the church was brought from St Etheldreda's church at Histon; also to be seen is a 600 year old bell (disused) and memorials to the Cotton family.

When the well-loved teacher Mrs Gwen Ruddle MBE retired from the village school after some 39 years in 1978, the village fought but lost the battle against the Local Education Authority's intention to cease to maintain or provide education in the parish. However, residents never gave up their commitment and the project made national and international headlines when they were assisted by an un-named person in their purchase of the building from the Church of England. However, the Parent Co-operative gave up the struggle to run the school in July 1997 due to the lack of children. It is now run privately.

The original windmill at Madingley was blown down in July 1909. The mill still standing was brought from Ellington, near

Huntingdon as a replacement and was re-erected by Mr C. Ison of Histon in 1935–6. This project was paid for by Mr Ambrose Harding of Madingley Hall. The windmill was restored in 1996 and now has sails.

The Co-op grocery, the baker and the butcher have not been seen delivering in the village for well over two decades; and the typically small village post office closed its doors in 1987. Alas, too, the blacksmith's shop was pulled down together with five cottages in the mid 1970s to make way for new bungalows in High Street. Other changes in the village have brought about the loss of four farms (Middle Farm, New Farm, Highfields and High Arden). The surviving two are Burnt Farm and Home Farm. The housing development at Granary Court was partly created from some old barns on Home Farm. Beck Brook Farm came onto the scene in the early 1980s.

The village hall was built by Colonel Harding in 1937. It was used as a NAAFI for the troops stationed at Madingley Hall during the Second World War. The committee paid the University a peppercorn rent of £1 per annum. The Village Hall Management Committee bought the hall from the University of Cambridge in 1993 for £5,000 and with the help of grants from South Cambridgeshire District Council and English Heritage the leaking half of the roof was re-thatched.

In 1960 the University of Cambridge created a small Ornithological Field Station, as a sub-department of the Department of Zoology in Cambridge. It has been altered a lot during the last few years and is now a big department with many new buildings.

International history is reflected in Madingley by way of the Cambridge American Cemetery and Memorial depicting the conflicts of the Second World War. The 30.5 acres of land, donated by the University of Cambridge, are situated on a gentle slope overlooking the East Anglian countryside towards Ely Cathedral.

🍁 MAXEY

Maxey village has a heritage steeped in history. Many of its quaint stone buildings were built hundreds of years ago and a team of archaeologists have discovered that the area contains relics of the Neolithic age including the only polished-stone axe to be excavated in England this century.

The parish church of St Peter was built in about AD 1113, in order to serve the needs of three hamlets: Maxey, Lolham and Nunton. The Lady Chapel was built in 1367. On the south wall of the chapel is a wooden plaque recording Mary Walsham's legacy. She died in 1745 and left £100, the interest from which was to be distributed to the poor of the parish in bread or money, as the minister and churchwardens thought desirable.

The altar is an oak table and scribbled underneath in pencil is 'John Francis Hardy made the table in December 1826'. The church has six fine sounding bells.

The present day Castle Farm was once 'Maxey Castle'. Margaret Beaufort, mother of Henry VII, resided here, presiding over the Deepings as lady of the manor in the year 1458.

In recent years one of the major changes in the village was the closing of the Maxey primary school and the transfer of pupils to the nearby village school at Northborough. The school was bought by the villagers and is now used as Maxey Community Centre.

The village is practically surrounded by water, with old gravel workings which have been well landscaped, giving some very pleasant waterside walks.

🍁 MELBOURN

Melbourn is situated to the east of the A10 between Royston and Cambridge. It has about 1,800 houses.

It has been suggested that Melbourn meant 'Melda's river'. Melda lived in Anglo-Saxon days at the Bury. It was the largest and most important house in the village. On the site springs a stream, which in 1086 ran nine mills, none of which are left today.

In 1690 William Ayloffe provided a free school for the children of Melbourn. This was held above the south porch of the church. Much later, in 1818, John Trigg left a large sum of money in his will for Melbourn children's education. This helped to found the primary school which is still in use today.

All Saints' church standing at the cross is of Norman origin. It was badly damaged during the Reformation and was subsequently repaired and rebuilt where necessary. One panel of the font still shows Norman arcading work.

The United Reformed church in Orchard Road was originally the Meeting House built in 1720. It is one of the oldest of its type in the country.

Lordship Farm, once known as Argentine Manor, was mentioned in the Domesday Book. Parts of the existing house in the High Street are 800 years old and there is still a Norman well in the cellar.

Further along the High Street are 'Sheeps Head Row' cottages. They were named this by a coach driver, who said that every time he drove through Melbourn with the mail, a head would appear from the upper window of each cottage. They looked, he said, like a row of sheep's heads hanging outside a butcher's shop!

There is a rare fire engine house in Station Road, built in 1847. This has been renovated on the instructions of the Parish Council and the original wording on the doors reinstated.

Melbourn today is a thriving community. It has a village college that serves 13 villages, its buildings used for a variety of activities. Melbourn has only three pubs now, but at one time, when the village was approximately half of its present size, it sported 20 pubs! It has all the shops necessary for its day-to-day needs. The industrial estate to the south of the village is now well established and the newer science park towards the north end is rapidly filling up with both established and new companies.

🍁 Meldreth

The village of Meldreth lies nine miles south west of Cambridge. The river Mel, a tributary of the Rhee later to become the Cam, runs through the village. In the past Meldreth was a thriving fruit growing area and special mention must be made of the Meldreth greengage, renowned for its flavour. Today arable farming has taken over from the orchards.

Holy Trinity church has stood, on the same site as an earlier wooden one, for almost 500 years. In the tower there are eight bells, the earliest dated 1617 and the newest 1968. Campanologists from all over the world visit this famous peal.

At one time there were several manors and watermills, of these Topcliffe's Mill still remains. In recent years it has been partially restored. There were few large houses and most of the population lived in small thatched cottages made of lath, plaster and clunch. Today's residents mostly live in modern houses with a sprinklng of old world properties. Workers commute to Cambridge, London and other distant places although a few work in the village where there is one large factory and several smaller enterprises.

Village celebrities include Andrew Marvell, the 17th century poet, who lived at the Court and wrote some of his poems there in the oak room. The niece of Neville Chamberlain lived at the Gables and in the same house many years before that a young son murdered his mother.

Under a large chestnut tree on Marvell's Green stand the stocks and whipping post last used in the 1860s. Beside them can be seen the stone base of an ancient praying cross. Meldreth Manor (the Manor of Streets) was given by the owners in the early 1960s to the Spastics Society who built in the grounds a residential school for 120 multi-handicapped children.

The population today is approximately 1,800 and well served by several shops, post office, primary school, village hall and public transport. In Victorian days there were six public houses but today only one remains. One of these pubs, near the church, belonged to a local brewery (Jarmans) and this house may well have been the guildhall as it still contains a dragon beam. Although this attractive village with a long history has seen many changes in recent years it still retains a rural atmosphere and strong community spirit.

❦ MEPAL

Mepal today is a small agricultural fenland village lying about half a mile off the Fen Trunk Road between Chatteris and Ely. Ireton's Way leads north to Chatteris, built to improve communications by Oliver Cromwell's engineers under General Ireton, straight as an ancient Roman road, over the Old and New Bedford Rivers.

The rivers were part of Vermuyden's fen drainage system – the Old Bedford being cut before the Civil War and the New Bedford, or Hundred Foot Drain, after it. The washes, which lie between the two, act as grazing fields in the summer and, becoming inundated by flood water in winter, are a natural refuge for wildfowl. The Gault Hole from which clay used to be dug for brickmaking, lies to the west of the village. The hole, now marshy, is a nesting place for swans and herons can be seen there occasionally.

The fens to the north of the village used to be frozen over for 4–8 weeks annually and local competition was fierce in the Ice Skating Championships, speed not style being essential!

South of the village lies the area known as Mepal Airfield. Now farmland, the 75th RNZAF Squadron flew Stirlings and Lancasters operationally during the Second World War and still retain affectionate links with local people. After the war the airfield briefly served as a Thor missile base.

One of Vermuyden's adventurers, James Fortrey, built Fortrey Hall, 'a commodious habitation', on the riverside, to which he retired when James II was exiled. The Hall had its own bridge over the Old Bedford River, and was said to be just a day's walk away from Ely

Cathedral for the monks on pilgrimage from Ramsey and Thorney.

Mepal is not mentioned in the Domesday Book, but St Mary's church, which has neither steeple nor tower, can be dated to the 12th century, and there are mentions of 'Mephale' in the Ely Diocese records from 1132.

One hundred years ago there were five public houses and a brewery in the village, today only one remains – the Three Pickerels. Near this pub is a farm, one of whose outbuildings has the date 1765 built into the brickwork. This was one of the sheds surrounding the old Market Place, which was later known as Cluncher's Yard when clunch was quarried from the river bank and stored there before being ferried away by barge.

The village school was built in 1874 to accommodate some 80 children of varying ages. Attendance would seem to have been erratic depending on agricultural requirements for 'hands' and, during bad weather, the passage of the ferry boat across the marshes. A modern school was built in 1966 some 100 yards away in Brangehill. The old building with its lovely windows and inherent memories of children's coats drying by the fire has been acquired as the village hall.

Opposite is a small village green where the local WI have erected a village sign depicting Vermuyden's wooden bridge with grazing sheep. The other, larger, village green is the scene of the continuing annual Mepal Feast in September.

🍁 MERESIDE

Mereside is now technically a hamlet, as it has neither church nor school. The old Baptist chapel has been renovated into two private homes, and the local children are 'bussed' to school.

Set in agricultural country, this area is rich fenland, with few trees but many waterways. Sugar beet, potatoes and wheat are the main crops, though at onion time the aroma from the fields is quite savoury.

Once, all the inhabitants either worked on the large farms or rented County Council smallholdings, now the majority travel to the towns for work.

The through road with houses on either side, which once hummed only with tractors and associated farm vehicles, now has to contend with commuter cars hurrying to work, and container lorries, servicing the rapidly increasing population's needs.

🍁 MILTON

In the 1920s, Milton was an interesting community of about 500 adults and children. It had its own school which bore the date 1836, the children being divided into three classes of about 30 children in each class.

Work was plentiful as there were several farms and, at busy times of the year, the workers helped out on each other's farms to get the crops planted and harvested. Gravel was dug and large gravel pits formed. Another company manufactured roof tiles. There were two nurseries, one specialising in tomatoes and cucumbers, the other selling bedding plants, general garden plants and seeds which were sent all over the country as a result of orders from their catalogue. A flourishing laundry business was carried on by the Goodin family. It is no longer in existence, having closed in 1990.

Milton had its share of characters, one being Vashti Wilkin who, not so very long ago, was a tower of strength to the village wives and the first to be sent for on the occasion of a birth. Time meant nothing to her as she would turn out whatever the hour and be prepared to stay however long the labour. It is said she was also there at life's end, helping with the laying out of the dead and the comfort of the bereaved. These services were given and no payment was expected by her. A community such as Milton also required a blacksmith as horses were used on the land. Mr Butcher filled this position, having his forge in the centre of the village near the pond and water pump.

Baitsbite Lock, Milton

He must have been a stalwart of the church as he was a verger, stoked the boilers, rang the bells, wound the church clock and blew the organ bellows, whilst his wife kept the church clean.

The second Sunday in May was Feast Sunday, being quite a highlight of the year for the residents, as Thurston's Amusements arrived, bringing the Gallopers, or Sedgewick's Ark, together with sideshows of quoits, darts and coconut shies. A set of swinging boats was an essential part of the show.

In times past, Milton had several thatched cottages but now there are only four, two in Church Lane, one in Fen Road and another at Baitsbite Lock. The church has quaint gargoyles on its 13th century tower. Throughout its history the church has featured prominently in village life and today there has been much effort and thought given to form the Children's Hospice in the house which was the old rectory.

Baitsbite was renovated in 1989 and a new style of automatic

162

guillotine lockgates installed. This has been depicted on the village sign. In the opinion of many, the new lockgates have spoilt the previous prettiness of the scene.

Milton today is very different from the 1920s as high-technology science is undertaken on the Milton Science Park. The village was earmarked a few years ago for housing development and this has now been completed. A supermarket was opened on the edge of the village in 1989, and a sports/playing field, which is now in constant use, was donated. Today's approximate population is 4,300.

In 1993 South Cambridgeshire District Council opened the Milton Country Park on the former gravel pits. This has proved a splendid amenity. Work is ongoing to create an ideal habitat for wildlife. School parties are encouraged and there is a very informative Visitors' Centre. The Park Ranger organises interesting walks and events throughout the year.

The village maintains a lively community spirit with many sporting and social activities centred around church, community centre and the country park.

🍁 MURROW

The original settlement of Murrow dates back to Roman times and existed on high land where a road was built along a bank. This was long before the draining of the fens.

In the first half of the 20th century, the village was inhabited almost entirely by railway and land workers. But the railway, once famous for its one of only two 'diamond crossings', where the Midland and Great Northern crossed the London and North Eastern, is now closed. There were two stations and, daily, fresh produce, fruit, vegetables and grain were brought to the station in horse-drawn wagons, to be taken by rail to markets all over the country.

With modern machinery, fewer men are needed for working the land, and so there is less casual work for the women, strawberry picking and spring flowers being the only things locally needing such labour. They even have machines for hoeing sugar beet seedlings! Therefore more and more people travel by car to nearby towns and cities, to work in offices, shops and factories.

There is a Methodist chapel and a church, but regular congregations are small, though the villagers would be loathe to see either close. The church is unique in that the altar is at its north end. It was built in 1857 as a chapel of ease, and is called Corpus Christi.

At one time there was a total of five public houses, but this has dwindled down to one now, the Bell.

In 1978 a tract of land was acquired by the villagers to lay a playing field. To pay for the general upkeep of the field, a Gala Week is held annually in July with functions for the entire population to participate in.

🍁 NEWBOROUGH & BOROUGH FEN

The parish of Newborough is very new, having been formed in 1823. The church, dedicated to St Bartholomew, was erected in 1830. The Church of England school dates back to 1852. The money came from the proceeds realised from the sale of part of Borough Fen estate at the time of the enclosures in 1822. Around the church are the oldest houses. The school, of course, has been extended with all modern improvements. At the turn of the century a few new houses were built, and after the First World War some council homes were added. After the Second World War a large council estate was built, then private estates started springing up, so that the village has grown considerably.

Newborough is a very large and scattered parish, and includes a hamlet called Milking Nook, approximately a mile away from the village. This is easily as old as the main village and got its name because in the 18th and 19th centuries farmers from neighbouring villages grazed their animals there. Each village had their own

164

droves, ie Barnack, Northborough, Bainton and Glinton. These roads still exist today, but bear no relevance to their situation.

Agriculture really is the only local industry and the area is made up of a few large farms, but is also dotted with smaller ones, where enterprising families have struggled to get a living.

On the southern and south western boundary runs the ancient Roman Car Dyke, which is unspoilt and a haven for wildlife.

Borough Fen consists of around 3,000 acres, and was originally waste and common land belonging to the Abbey of Peterborough. Then by Act of Parliament in 1812, land was allotted to the common land tenants, but some was sold for drainage expenses. This was the first drainage to take place. The inhabitants at this time occupied a few farmhouses and scattered cottages. In 1920, however, the Soke of Peterborough County Council bought most of the land for smallholdings, chiefly for ex-servicemen.

The gem of Borough Fen is the Duck Decoy. The earliest reference is in 1670, when the Decoyman (Mr Williams) was granted permission to pierce the river Welland to lead water to his decoy pond. The Decoy was continuously managed by the Williams family until the death of Billy Williams in 1958, who was well known in the district. In 1951 the Wildfowl Trust undertook the financial responsibility of ringing the ducks that are caught, instead of killing them and the decoy is the oldest of the few decoys surviving.

🍁 NEWNHAM

Until the middle of the last century, Newnham had very few buildings, most of which were in Newnham Road and around the mill. It was not until the end of the 19th century that further building began and Newnham grew as we know it today. Towards the latter part of the 13th century, a Carmelite friary existed somewhere near the mill, which seems to have been a focal point for centuries. The mill race was supposed to have been cut before the Domesday

Book to serve the mill. The mill as we see it now, was rebuilt after a fire in 1853. In 1977 it was refurbished without losing its character, now being the restaurant known as 'Sweeney Todd'.

When in 1882 the Fellows of the colleges at Cambridge were allowed to marry, a lot of big houses were built for them and their families, and smaller houses were built for the college servants and employees. The infant school, first mentioned in 1874, was situated where the petrol station is now sited. Newnham Croft School, as it is now known, was moved to its present position in 1925.

Next to the petrol station are the Perse Almshouses, re-erected in 1886. In the will of Stephen Perse MD, Fellow of Gonville & Caius, who died in 1625, money was left for 'Six several low tenements of one room apiece to be built near his free school, for six several Almsfolk, poor, aged and unmarried women, to be at least over 40 years and parishioners of St Edward's, St Michael's or St Benet's. The appointments to be made by the Master of Caius and some fellows . . . each inhabitant to receive £26 per annum.'

The Malting House, one of Newnham's landmarks, was rebuilt in its present form a few years before the First World War. The original building is believed to have been built 100 years beforehand. The very narrow Maltings Lane leads right to Ridley Hall, the theological college, and left to Church Rate Walk. With its old cottages and narrow lane it is completely unspoiled and beautiful.

The first church in Newnham was a wooden building which stood between the present church and vicarage. It was a mission church in the parish of Grantchester. In 1885 the parish room, now a flourishing community centre, with two rooms above it, was built: and in 1889 the vicarage for the curate was completed. The foundation stone for the present church was laid in 1900, and on St Mark's Day in 1901 the church was dedicated by the Bishop of Ely. But it was not until 1918 that St Mark's became a separate parish.

As for the present? A lot of infilling has taken place of course, but on the whole, looking at old photographs, Newnham Croft has changed little. Cows and horses are still grazing on Sheeps Green, which in the spring looks like a yellow carpet when covered with buttercups. There are still many old trees and those that were destroyed by storms have been replaced by new ones.

🍁 NEWTON

Newton is a delightful small village in South Cambridgeshire. It has a long recorded history having been first mentioned in a document of AD 975 and there is evidence of even earlier, Romano-British, occupation of the area.

In medieval times most of the land was owned by the monks of Ely. Newton was one of 33 Ely manors and Newton people had to produce a quota of food for the monks as well as meeting other feudal obligations. The manor court ruled the village and there was a manor farmhouse here.

After the Dissolution of the Monasteries the manor passed to the Dean and Chapter of Ely Cathedral. They leased the manor to local men like the farmer John Swan in the 16th century and to others, such as Dr John Hills, a Canon of Ely, and Dr Gideon Harvey of Middlesex, a physician, during the 17th century. Later, the manor lease passed to the Hurrell family, a member of which was able to buy the reversion of the lease in the mid 19th century. The estate remains with a member of the Hurrell family to this day.

Agriculture remained almost the only source of employment for the men of the village well into the 20th century. Only domestic work and seasonal field work was available to women.

By the second half of the 19th century there were two substantial houses in Newton. One, Newton Hall, was built in the 1850s by a local landowning family, the Pembertons. The other was the home of the Hurrell family. At about the time of the purchase of the freehold of the estate, the purchaser, William Hurrell, demolished the old manor farmhouse and, in its place, built a new house in the Victorian-Tudor style and called it The Manor.

167

The Hurrell family had a good reputation for concern for the welfare of village people and, by the 1890s, had established evening classes in basic subjects. At about this time a bachelor son of the family, Harold Hurrell, became very interested in the Arts and Crafts movement of the time. He established a Metalwork Evening School in Newton which flourished for several decades. An official report of the time gives a good indication of its standing and importance. Austin Keen, Education Secretary for Cambridgeshire County Council, wrote in 1902: 'The grandest work in this direction that I know of is done by Mr Hurrell of Newton. Last year the Newton school turned out £219 worth of metalwork, producing a substantial profit for the workers. This occupies six months of the year. As soon as the spring is fairly in, the school is closed and the men are encouraged to work on the gardens and allotments. Nor is the school simply a manufacturing or producing one; the educational side of the work is by no means neglected. The young men are systematically taught drawing and designing especially as applied to their repousse work, forging, soldering, metal plating and enamelling. It is intensely interesting to see a group of agricultural labourers collectively working out the details of an elaborate design in which probably each of the branches above-mentioned is illustrated and applied – all of them exercising an intelligent knowledge of the detailed drawings and a splendid enthusiasm in translating them into metal form. For such men life has an additional significance to anything the day school ever imparted.'

As early as the mid 1890s work was being exhibited in London and the prestigious *Studio* magazine reported on and named Newton work and craftsmen.

In many households in Newton, especially in those of older people, there are treasured articles of worked copper which were made by their friends and relatives in the Metalwork School. It continued to function until the 1940s. As a result of the regular London exhibitions Newton work was widely known and orders were executed for people all over the country. The work included inn

168

signs, ecclesiastical objects, lamps, vases, war memorials and much else. A copper lamp, made in the school, was put up at the crossroads as a memorial to Harold Hurrell after his death in the 1920s.

Although Newton remains a small village it continues to have agreeable links with a wider area as it had in the days of the Metalwork School. Every year talented local residents write and produce a pantomime, which runs to five performances and is seen by many people who come from beyond the village. Every day visitors from afar visit the village pub, the Queens Head, a former coaching inn, on the old turnpike road from Cambridge to Ware.

St Margaret's church was consecrated in 1346, although there is evidence that prior to that, as a chapel, it had been a place of worship for some time. The earliest part of the building, the short nave, dates back to the beginning of the 13th century. In the early spring the churchyard, with its carpet of snowdrops and aconites attracts many visitors.

The village school, which was situated at the crossroads, was closed in the 1960s and children now receive their primary education in Harston. Also situated at the crossroads are the village rooms, which house the village hall (used for many activities) and the Sports and Social Club and, a few yards away, in Harston Road, is Newton's only shop, which includes the post office.

Local people have a justifiable sense of pride in Newton.

🍁 NEWTON IN THE ISLE

Situated in the north of the county this Newton is a small village just in Cambridgeshire, but on the borders of Lincolnshire and Norfolk.

Passing through on the B1165, about four miles from Wisbech, on the main road through the village you will see the village sign.

The figure on the sign is of Sir John Colvile, the most famous of the Colviles, who were the lords of the manor of Newton since the time of the Norman Conquest. Sir John fought at the Battle of Agincourt with King Henry V. He founded the college or chantry called the Chapel of St Mary in the Marsh or 'Capella Maris' in 1403 and endowed it with £40 per annum to maintain four chaplains, four clerks and ten poor men. The college depicted on the sign stood on the old Roman bank near to the old rectory. Strange to think the sea came so close.

The white lion rampant has been part of the Colvile coat of arms since 1280. The six bells denote the six bells on St James' parish church, built in the 13th century. On the right hand side of the sign there is a woad plant. Woad was grown to the end of the 19th century in Newton and was probably pressed in the woad mill at Parson Drove. In the present day, one local pub is called the Woadman's Arms and the other the White Lion. The latter has the lion rampant as its sign.

The original Hall in Newton had a series of sitting rooms opening into each other to form a gallery. Over the mantelpiece in the servants' hall was a sign which said 'Whosoever sits down and says not Grace, sits down a fool and gets up an ass'. Only the cellars remain under the present Hall – rebuilt in 1807.

The first school was built on glebe land in 1853 and financed by the church. By 1928 it was forced to give up the struggle against inflation and poor conditions. The County Council took over and built a new school, opened in 1930 and called The Colvile School.

The new school existed for 57 happy years but because of the falling birthrate and financial cutbacks, sadly it has closed and the name of Colvile has faded out, though there is still a Colvile Road in the village.

🍁 NORTHBOROUGH

The village of Northborough is situated on the A15, seven miles north of Peterborough. Northborough was first mentioned in the 12th century Survey of Northamptonshire, although there is evidence of an earlier settlement.

Northborough village

Originally, the village was built round the church and manor house, this being the oldest part of the present village, and boasts many fine stone and thatched cottages.

The manor house, or Northborough Castle as it is known today, is believed to have been built by the de la Mare family around the mid 14th century. The manor was bought in 1563 by James Claypole and it is through this family that the village was to become connected with Oliver Cromwell due to the marriage of his daughter Elizabeth to John Claypole. Since these early times, the manor has been owned by several families and at present is privately owned.

The parish church of St Andrew has been described as 'a monument of disappointed hopes and unaccomplished ambitions', giving the impression of being 'more curious than beautiful'. This is due to the mixture of architectural styles from the 12th to 14th centuries, each period of building being incomplete, probably due to lack of funds. An interesting part of the church is its Norman bell-

171

cote which is one of three within the local area. There are only two bells, one dated between 1359 and 1380 and the other dated 1611. Once again the village link to Oliver Cromwell is apparent as his wife was buried here on 19th November 1665. St Andrew's also provides a resting place for Martha, widow of John Clare the poet (who lived in the village for 10 years). As well as the parish church the village also has a Methodist chapel which was built in 1869.

Over the years there have been several public houses and drinking places, two of the better known being the Cuckoo Inn, which is now sadly only remembered as a bus stop, and the Packhorse, which is the only existing public house. The Cuckoo Inn and the Packhorse were once village shops as well.

The original school was built around 1877 and can still be seen opposite the manor; this is now a private dwelling. The new school was built in 1966 to accommodate the growth in population and the merger of Maxey and Northborough schools in 1969.

To show that Northborough once was a village with influence, during the late 13th century an annual fayre was held on 14th August. This fayre was surrendered by Geoffrey de la Mare, Lord of the Manor, due to the injury it caused to the Abbot of Peterborough's fayre. Nowadays this has been replaced by an annual family day.

🍁 OAKINGTON

The name Oakington – Hockington in the Domesday Book – has nothing to do with oak trees but is a corruption of 'Hoca's tun'. The discovery, in 1928, of three Anglo-Saxon skeletons buried in shallow graves, one of them with a shield over its shattered skull, suggests that this was the site of an ancient battlefield. The part played by more recent warriors, RAF Oakington in the Second World War, is recognised by a bas relief of a bomber flying across a blue sky on the village sign.

The village today is roughly centred on the parish church of St

Andrew, 13th century with a 12th century nave. The fabric is in excellent condition, almost all the repair work having been done during the last 20 years by enthusiastic church members and their families. The church has not, however, always been in such good heart and indeed, in 1683, the Bishop described the parish of Oakington as 'the most evil' and 'most full of vice' in his diocese. Presumably this was because most of the parishioners refused to go to church at all, preferring to listen to itinerant preachers in the great barns of East Anglian farmers. For Oakington lies in the heart of Cromwell country and throughout the 17th century was a stronghold of religious independence.

The most famous of the dissenters was the Congregationalist Francis Holcroft, known as 'The Apostle of East Anglia'. He was buried in 1692 just outside Oakington churchyard by the side of his assistant Joseph Oddy and Henry Osland, the pastor of the first Congregationalist church in the area. For many years visitors to the 'Oakington Graves' have assumed that the dissenters had been denied burial in sanctified ground, but recent research has shown that the Nonconformists had bought a field adjoining the churchyard as a cemetery of their own.

At the extreme north east of the parish boundary is the railway line from March to Cambridge. It came to the small village of Oakington in 1846 because the much larger village of Cottenham wanted nothing to do with it. As a result, market gardeners from the fenlands beyond had to bring all their apples, cabbages, strawberries, asparagus and cut flowers to the goods yard at Oakington which also handled great numbers of milk churns and mountains of domestic coal. Sadly the station was closed down in 1970 and today the only trains passing through are gravel trains from pits originally opened up to provide jobs for unemployed farm labourers.

No description of Oakington would be complete without a mention of one of the oldest villagers, the white-bearded 'Snowy' Farr. Snowy, a retired roadman, has devoted his energies to raising money for charity by exhibiting his collection of pet animals with whom he has an uncanny rapport. He can often be seen in the village, immaculate in a scarlet guardsman's tunic, leather gaiters and a silk top hat, riding a flag-bedecked tractor or pedalling an old, gaily painted ice-cream tricycle on his way to the Saturday market at Cambridge or to other charitable events.

🍁 THE OFFORDS

The Offords are comprised of Offord Cluny and Offord Darcy. Offord Cluny has a current population of 490 compared with 170 in 1801. Before the Domesday survey in 1086 Arnulf de Hesding made the gift of an estate in the village to the Abbey of Cluny, a town in Burgundy, France. When the monks left after 300 years, the name remained. Offord Darcy has a population of 790 today, compared with 156 in 1801, and owes its name to the Darcy family who held land there in 1220.

The Horseshoe, Offord Darcy

Each village has its own church though they were united in one parish in 1976. All Saints' in Offord Cluny was built in the 13th century and St Peter's, Offord Darcy in 1130. Services are held mainly in All Saints' as St Peter's is designated a redundant church. There is a Baptist church in Offord Darcy. Also in Offord Darcy are the Church Rooms, which are available for hire and widely used by various organisations. Other features of the villages are Offord Cluny Manor House built in 1704 and Darcy Manor built in 1607. The old school opened in 1875 and was replaced in 1988 by a new school on the existing site.

The railway was constructed in 1850. The main employers in the villages are grain merchants and haulage. Farming, mostly arable, also plays an important part in the life of the community.

Each village also has its own public house. Offord Cluny has a riding school, fruiterer and greengrocer. Offord Darcy has a hairdresser's and a motor works. The village hall, which was opened in 1981, is a central meeting place and serves both villages.

The two parishes have joined together to purchase land for a new Millennium Green. The main leisure activities are fishing, boating, canoeing, riding, rambling, archery, and the river attracts many visitors to the villages during the summer.

🍁 ORTON LONGUEVILLE

A village once occupied by the Romans and now grown to accommodate the increasing population of Peterborough, it nevertheless retains its old world charm and history. Orton Longueville is mentioned in the Domesday Book.

Roman remains of the 2nd and 4th centuries were discovered in 1907 and in the 1960s a basilica was found and now lies under a modern housing estate, namely Orton Malborne.

The village street meanders for about 700 metres ending at the southern end at a non-motorised lane, by the name of Moggeswell!

Also at this end is a large village green complete with a magnificent chestnut tree but, unfortunately, no blacksmith.

The church of the Holy Trinity is c1240. It still retains its sanctus bell and also a bell cast in Plantagenet times. There is a splendid wall painting from the 16th century and a very fine sculpture of Lady Mary Seymour of Chantrey. One must not forget the stone effigy of an armoured knight.

Standing adjacent to the church is Orton Hall built by the then Marquis of Huntly and Aboyne and occupied by that family for many years. It was built of the famous Barnack ragstone from the nearby Barnack quarry; many of the houses in the village and also the church are built of the same stone. The Hall was extended in 1855. The avenue leading up to the hall is flanked by magnificent Wellingtonia trees which are of course protected. The Hall is now a hotel complex.

Although Orton Longueville is encircled by modern housing, one can still wander through the village and see interesting buildings of yesteryear.

🍁 ORTON WATERVILLE

Orton Waterville lies just off the A605, three miles west of Peterborough and two miles east of the A1.

Orton, an abbreviation of Overton, means 'farm on the slope or hill'. After the Norman Conquest the Waterville family owned the manors of Overton and Thorpe as tenants to the Abbots of Peterborough, and gave their name to the village.

In 1922 a local historian, W.T. Mellows, stated: 'Overton Waterville is an unspoilt medieval village. The church, the manor house and the ancient homesteads remain. Traces of the open field system may still be recognised in the lands at the back of the town street. Long may it continue as a place of delight to the lover of antiquity, a surviving example of the village of our forefathers.'

Early in the 16th century the manor belonged to the warden and scholars of Pembroke College.

In 1801 the population was 270, in 1931 it was 315. However the proximity of Orton Waterville to Peterborough led to the development of land to the east of the village – Lady Lodge estate. By 1971 the population was 1,300 and by 1996 it was 9,950. The parish now encompasses the new development areas of Orton Brimbles, Orton Wistow and Orton Southgate.

There are a number of interesting houses, some of them thatched. Roman relics found here are held in Peterborough Museum. Manor Farm and some parts of the Rectory date from the Elizabethan era. A 15th century dovecote stands in the garden.

The village church still retains some Norfolk work but it was largely rebuilt in the Early English period and added to about a century later. One of its doors and the oak pulpit have been here since the reign of Elizabeth I. The pulpit is magnificent. Richly carved it rises from a tapered base above a frieze of foliage beautifully decorated with ornamental arches supported by pilasters, above which are intricately carved panels flanked by quaint figures. The font is 500 years old. The communion table and two beautiful inlaid chairs date from the 17th century. The Methodist chapel dates from 1880 and is small but beautiful.

The old village is now a conservation area within the new Orton Township and part of the city of Peterborough.

🍁 ORWELL

In common with almost every other village in the country, Orwell has changed very much since the Second World War when it was a predominantly agricultural area.

Changes have come in the look of the village. Before the Second World War almost all of the cottages were built of the local chalk known as clunch which from time immemorial had been quarried

The Old School, Orwell

from the large pit behind the parish church. To preserve it clunch had to be whitewashed regularly. Therefore Orwell presented a picture, apart from the few houses built of the local 'Cambridge white' brick, of white dwellings covered with thatched roofs. Straw was plentiful and the thatcher lived in the village. Now very few residents can afford to have thatching done and the thatcher would have to be brought in to the village and would probably use Norfolk reeds instead of Orwell straw.

At the time of the Domesday Book, Orwell had 20 families and by 1801 there were 375 inhabitants. The population rose sharply by 1870 to 800 because of the coprolite digging which was carried out quite extensively here and in neighbouring villages.

In 1930 the first council houses were built and they were followed at regular intervals before and after the war by further council building, the last being a quite substantial estate known as Meadowcraft Way, built on what was always known as the Mash, which was a water-logged marsh in 1590.

The church of St Andrew is mostly built of clunch and field stones. The nave and chancel date from about 1200 and the tower is older still. On the south wall of the chancel is a memorial to a rector, Jeremiah Radcliffe, who was one of the translators of the Authorised version of the Bible in 1611.

On St Thomas' Day, a little group of widows, known as 'Goodies', used to call on selected houses for hoped for gifts and would also receive a noble (6s 8d) from the rector. This was left by one of the charities. Another charity, the Colbatch and Hooper, gave an allowance to apprentices and, in restructured form, still does, as well as giving a generous allowance to those students going on to higher education.

Schooling has been available for Orwell children since the 16th century and Petersfield Church of England Primary School, built in 1965, now serves Orwell, Arrington, Wimpole and Croydon.

Orwell was one of the most important centres of religious dissent in the county during the 17th century, with a strong Congregationalist community. Methodism had taken over by the 19th century and until the last decades of the 20th century allegiance to either the Methodist Church or the Church of England produced sharp social divisions in the village. Happily, interdenominational services are now often held, either at St Andrew's or in the Methodist church, rebuilt in 1909, and a Roman Catholic service is also held in the parish church once a month. In 1959 the Bicentenary of Methodist preaching in the Cambridge Circuit was celebrated in Orwell in the largest barn in the village, at West Farm, which is now converted into dwellings.

Buildings on other farms were also converted into homes in the 1960s and the number of farmers resident in the village has reduced to three. Several shops have closed, including a butcher's shop which had traded for nearly 250 years, and the village now has just one shop, a flourishing general store and post office, rebuilt in 1998 with an in-store bakery, and a unisex hairdressing salon. Volac, the animal feedstuffs company in Fishers Lane, employs a number of local people and an increasing number of residents are either retired or work from home; most Orwellians, however, commute to Cambridge, Royston or the London area and a few work in the village. The Parish Council publishes a quarterly magazine, the *Orwell Bulletin*, which gives news of the activities of the many societies which foster community spirit in this most sociable village.

🍁 OVER

Over is a fenland edge settlement by the river Ouse, eleven miles north west of Cambridge. The name, meaning 'bank of the river', is of Saxon origin. In the Middle Ages, Over was one of the largest villages in Cambridgeshire, with a market place opposite the church.

In 1254 the Bishop of Ely granted a licence to build the church. The stone seats round the wall still exist and this custom originated the phrase 'the weaker go to the wall'. After the porch was added in 1320, it became a meeting place for the villagers. It belonged to Ramsey Abbey until the reign of Henry VIII, when St Mary's church, its tithe and advowson were given to Trinity College, Cambridge. The church has a peal of eight bells and a medieval sanctus bell.

Water has ceased to flow through Over church gargoyles, which an East Anglian guide book describes as 'the most engaging gargoyles this side of Notre Dame de Paris'. Rupert Brooke obviously did not hold the people of Over in such high esteem as in a poem he wrote 'At Over they fling oaths at one'.

From the 10th century, woad was grown and sold in St Ives market, resulting in the cloth-dyeing industry and glove-making here, and eels and wildfowl were plentiful. Osiers growing by the river were used for basket-making. The villagers sabotaged the dykes being built by Vermuyden in 1630 to drain the fens, thinking they would lose their livelihood. Engineers built the Dutch-style houses still to be seen in Fen End and the High Street. Later, meat and dairy

Over village

products were taken to Cambridge market where, until 1914, Over set the price of butter by the yard.

The Town Hall was built in 1849 for £250 by Over Town Lands Trust on the site of a medieval Guild Hall. Until 1933 a chain ferry took horses and carts, and later, cars, across the river at Overcote to Needingworth. Now, at weekends, an average of 50 boats go along the river and through the lock which is now mechanised. The worst local disaster occurred in 1947 when the river bank burst and hundreds of acres of farmland were flooded. Villagers used to skate on the flooded fen fields and students came from Cambridge for the sport.

Some houses are built of yellow bricks, hand-made from the mid 19th century to 1931 in Longstanton Road. Many houses were clayed with clay from Mill Pits. The jettied house in West Street was built of wattle and daub.

Some fruit farms remain, growing plums, apples and pears, and nurseries growing pyrethrums and chrysanthemums.

181

A village sign was erected on the village green in July 1989. The WI organised the project and most of the work was done by local people. A day centre was opened in October 1989, providing care and a cooked midday meal from Monday to Saturday for up to 16 people. A community centre is scheduled to open in mid 1999. This will provide a purpose built centre for recreational and social use with adjacent facilities for football and cricket. The population has increased considerably to almost 3,000 due to new housing estates, and these days most people commute to Cambridge to work.

🍁 PAMPISFORD

The village lies seven miles south east of Cambridge and the nearest village is Sawston, which borders it to the north. The river Cam is on the south west boundary and the river Granta to the north east. The eastern boundary of the parish follows the Roman road north of Stumps Cross.

Pampisford grew around its High Street and agriculture was the main activity until the late 18th century. There were two manor houses, both owned by the same family.

In 1840 the Sawby family owned a brewery here and William was brewer maltster on the site north of Brewery Road. This site was selected for the excellent water found in the area. Latterly malt vinegar was produced at the factory until it closed and was subsequently redeveloped.

Pampisford Mill (now a private residence) stands on the river Granta; records show that since at least 1086 a mill has stood on this site. Originally grain was ground here, but in 1802 it was converted into a papermill, although milling of grain may have continued at the same time.

In 1893 the Easter Counties Leather Company purchased the mill and £500 was spent converting it into a power source for the leather works. Unfortunately by 1926 the company was in severe financial difficulties and so Charles Moore (an employee) took it over and revived the business. The firm is still run by the Moore family, now into its fourth generation.

The Dower House (which stands on the High Street) is the only medieval house in the village. When first built this would have been one of the most important buildings. It was probably built in 1455 and may have been the dower house to Sawston Hall.

There are three public houses in Pampisford. The White Horse (near the boundary with Sawston) was completely rebuilt after being demolished in 1937. The Chequers is on the corner of High Street and Brewery Road and is the oldest pub. Unfortunately in 1973 the thatch caught fire and was replaced by shingles. The Railway Inn is on the northern border near the A11, tucked away on a by-road and opposite Solo Park, a reclaimed building materials yard on the site of the old station which closed in 1967.

🍁 PARSON DROVE

It is reported and generally accepted that the village derives its name from the fact that the parson residing in the neighbouring village of Leverington walked along the mud road or 'drove' to take services in the village church.

The focal point of the village is the village green, one of the best to be found in Cambridgeshire. On the green near the Swan Inn is the building known as the cage. It was built in 1829, under the direction of John Peck, the village constable, as the village lock-up. It was also the pound and later housed the village fire engine. Parson Drove was the only village in the district to have its own fire engine. In 1897, to commemorate Queen Victoria's Diamond Jubilee, a clock tower was built onto the roof of the cage. Instead of numbers, letters spell 'VR SIXTY YEARS'. There are two oak trees nearby, planted to commemorate the Golden and Diamon Jubilees of Queen Victoria's reign. Facing the cage is the village sign which was erected in 1977 to mark Queen Elizabeth's Silver Jubilee.

Samuel Pepys spent a night at the Swan Inn to visit his relations. Unfortunately his horse was stolen and he was 'much troubled by gnats'. He was later to describe the village in his famous diary as 'a heathen place'.

The John Peck Society was formed in Parson Drove in 1998 to further the knowledge of John Peck and his contribution to the village. John Peck was a very prominent farmer who kept a day to day diary of events in his life from 1814 until his death in 1851. He came to live in Parson Drove in 1808 and resided at Inham Hall from 1811 until his death. Unfortunately Inham Hall no longer exits. John Peck was very much involved in the formation of the New North Level Main drain across the fen, and the building of Clough Cross sluice.

Woad, the plant from which a blue dye was obtained, was grown in the village. The woad mill was demolished in 1917 but there is still a farm called Woad Farm.

This must be one of the few small villages with two churches, and a chapel. One of the churches, St John's, goes back to the 11th century, and is taken care of by the Redundant Churches Trust, but brought to life at Christmas, when it is the scene of a delightful candlelit village carol service.

The village has altered greatly over the years with many new residents finding it a very friendly place. It has a general store, garage, butcher's, hairdressers, post office and three public houses which all serve meals. It also has a day centre for the elderly which serves the surrounding villages, adjoining the village primary school. There is a new surgery which also serves the surrounding villages, and a well used village hall and playing field.

🍁 PEAKIRK

The small village of Peakirk lies approximately seven miles north west of Peterborough.

At one end of the village behind Victorian houses, stands a timber workshop founded in 1890, a family firm which makes garden sheds etc. The business is still run by the grandson of the founder. This part of the village is known as the 'new end' as it mainly consists of houses built after the First World War. The solidly built police station is here and a few yards further on, for 31 years, stood the post office, which unfortunately closed in 1987. This building was once the Railway Inn. Behind the post office stands the Victorian station house. The railway line is still open for small diesel trains but the station itself closed in the 1960s.

The older part of the village has many fine stone houses, mostly Georgian. The village pub, the Ruddy Duck, once known as the Black Bull, is now the only surviving public house of three. Opposite lies the village hall built in 1974 with money raised by the villagers. The monument locally known as the 'Cross' was erected in 1904 by Edward James, a past rector.

By the church stands Chestnuts, a fine square Georgian house often mistaken for the rectory. The parish church dedicated to St Pega is the oldest building in Peakirk, but the foundations of the Hermitage to be found across the village green go back to the mists of time! The rediscovery of the wall paintings in 1949 has brought many visitors to the church. The rector now lives in Glinton and the rectory has become a family home.

The only thatched cottage in Peakirk faces the village green and now belongs to the Wildfowl Trust. The Waterfowl Gardens occupy the site of an old osier bed through which passed the ancient Car Dyke. In Roman times this was one of the chief waterways of East Anglia. Today, however, it is waterfowl which paddle the waterways. Another well-known waterway is the Folly Dyke, used by hundreds of fishermen. Crossing the Folly, you leave the parish and encroach onto the black soil of the fens.

🍁 PRICKWILLOW

Prickwillow is a small village of about 500 people built on the black fen, bounded to the north east by the river Lark and lying within the city of Ely, although four miles distant from it. Still surrounded by arable farmland the community is no longer entirely dependent on it as once it was.

First mentioned in 1251, Prickwillow did not emerge as a recognisable village settlement until the course of the river Ouse, which ran through its centre, was diverted into a straight cut between Queen Adelaide and Littleport in 1830. The river's higher bank became Main Street and buildings were erected from that time on the old river bed.

St Peter's church was rebuilt on wooden piles in 1866 in Gothic style and faced in flint. Above the altar blue roof-beams are painted with stars and its exquisite marble font is decorated with cherubs, shells and ropes of pearls. The present Baptist chapel was built in 1875. The Church of England school, completed in 1874, and the Methodist chapel (1894) are now both private homes. There is no cemetery because of the ongoing shrinkage of the peaty fen soil. The Victorian vicarage is a classic example of this soil shrinkage with a dozen steps added over time to reach its front door. Prickwillow lies well below sea level and its Drainage Engine Museum illustrates the efforts made to keep farmland and people safely above water.

🍁 PYMOOR

Pymoor is a small village in the parish of Little Downham and lies about six miles north of Ely. The name is spelled Pymore by the GPO, but all the old residents spell it Pymoor.

The land surrounding the village is very black fenland and very rich and fertile. The only grass field in the village is the playing and cricket field. Residents in Pymoor and along the banks of the Hundred Foot river worked mostly on farms, both men and women. In quite recent years the women used to chop the sugar beet out and then chop the ends off it with a curved hook. Some of the men worked on the banks of the river and digging the dykes around the fields. There was also wildfowling and punt gunning in the wash land on the other side of the river. Farmers would keep stock on the wash land during the summer, and in the winter these washes took the surplus water and were flooded. The washes stretch from Earith to Denver in Norfolk and are 21 miles long and approximately one mile wide. The RSPB now own about 1,850 acres of the washes and the Cambridgeshire Wildlife Trust approximately 250 acres.

Pymoor in years gone by had two or three windmills which were used for draining the land. In later years one windmill ground corn and was also a bakery. The miller had horses and carts going around the village and the outlying farmsteads and cottages delivering the freshly baked bread.

Pymoor had a unique school and church as they were built together in one building under the same roof. The school being at the roadway end, one had to pass through the school to enter the church. This was built out of the village along a public footpath halfway between Pymoor and Oxlode. Sadly Pymoor school, like many village schools, was closed in July 1981. The church struggled on with half the building but was finally closed on Christmas Day 1981. Pymoor still has one place of worship – the Methodist chapel, which was opened in 1954.

Close to Pymoor is the Hundred Foot Pumping Engine which pumps the water from the drain into the river. On that spot first stood a windmill, followed by a steam engine, a diesel engine and now the new one driven by electricity. The 'Poet Laureate of the Fens' was born at Pymoor Hill in 1794. He was William Harrison and was well known for many poems, one of which is on the Hundred Foot Pumping Engine today. It reads as follows:

'These Fens have oftimes been by Water drowned
Science a remedy in Water found
The power of Steam she said shall be employed
And the Destroyer by itself destroyed.'

QUEEN ADELAIDE

Queen Adelaide lies to the east of Ely on the B1382. It is a typical long street fen village and although it is quite separate and nearly two miles from Ely itself, it is regarded as being part of the city of Ely.

The village is divided into four by the main railway lines from Ely to Norwich, Peterborough and Kings Lynn which were opened in 1845, 1846 and 1847 respectively.

The present village dates back to the mid 19th century and takes its name from the Queen Adelaide public house which stood near to the river Ouse at the east end of the village. However, there are records of farms and dwellings in the vicinity as far back as AD 970.

Before the fens were drained, the area was covered with many small islands. Turbutsea Island, which was to the south of the present village, was where the monks of Ely landed when they stole the body of Saint Withburga from Dereham in order to bury her next to her sister Saint Etheldreda in Ely Monastery.

The monks would not recognise their island today as the site is covered by a sprawling factory which dominates the skyline of that part of the village. For more than 50 years, during the sugar beet harvest, the road through the village throbbed with the noise of tractor and lorry engines taking the raw beet to be processed, and the sickly, sweet smell hung heavily in the air over the village. Today the workers' houses have fallen down, the smell has gone and the factory has become a storage and distribution centre. Lorries still thunder down the main street of the village though, carrying their loads of fen potatoes, carrots and onions destined for the markets of the Midlands.

The river provides excellent fishing and is also used by the Cambridge University boat club for practice. A notable event was the 1944 Boat Race between Oxford and Cambridge. It was thought to be too dangerous to hold the race in London during the war so the stretch of river between Littleport bridge and Queen Adelaide bridge was used. Five thousand people watched Oxford win by three quarters of a length.

At one time Queen Adelaide, like most villages had a school, a shop and a church. Now these are all private houses. The church, dedicated to Saint Etheldreda, was erected in 1883 to replace a mission church. Standing as it does near the river, it was not unknown for couples to travel by boat to church to be married. It was closed in about 1968.

🍁 SAWSTON

The earliest record of the village of Sawston is found in Saxon times when there was a settlement called Salsingtune. By Domesday (1086) the village had three manors and 125 people.

Sawston's most notable historic event happened in 1553 when Princess Mary, soon to be queen, stayed the night at Sawston Hall when being pursued by her enemies. Tradition has it that she set out the next day dressed as a dairymaid riding behind her protector John Huddleston, the owner of Sawston Hall. On reaching high ground they looked back and saw flames and smoke rising from the Hall which had been fired by the Protestant mob. The Hall was badly damaged and later John Huddleston was granted material from the ruins of Cambridge Castle with which to rebuild his home. This Tudor mansion built in 1557 (with a priest hole and the traditional ghost!) is still standing today and is now a language school.

Many notable buildings remain from early days – Brook House, the oldest of all, dates from the 13th century, the Queen's Head pub from the 15th century and Ward House from the 16th century. Parts of the parish church date back to Norman times.

A custom from the 16th century has been upheld almost to the present day. This was a charity, instigated in his will by John Huntingdon, that every year two acres of his land should be sown with peas for the relief of the poor people in the village. The picking of the peas was allocated to a certain time on a certain day when the poor and needy would line the field. Nowadays the 'poor and needy' line the fields armed with plastic dustbin bags and take home the peas to fill their freezers!

Agriculture was naturally the main occupation of Sawston folk but in the 19th century Sawston expanded into an industrial village as many local industries were set up. The first successful business was the tannery set up by Thomas Evans, whose son later introduced the manufacture of chamois leather. Then came John Crampton who installed a printing works behind his shop. Edward Towgood, another big name, owned the paper mill and gained a wide reputation for the manufacture of the finest grades of paper. These industries are still very much alive today and account for a large proportion of the jobs available in the village. There is also an expanding industrial estate.

Sawston was the first village in England to have a village college, introduced by the educationalist Henry Morris. Many of the village activities centre round the village college which also has a wide adult education programme.

There is as yet no village hall, though one has been talked about for well over a hundred years! There is no cinema and no market but there is a health centre, a fire station, three churches, a good shopping centre and a more than adequate number of pubs! Although there is a tendency for villages to become dormitories for the nearest large town or city Sawston has maintained and is increasing its own identity and has indeed become a centre itself for many smaller surrounding villages.

🍁 SAWTRY

Sawtry (formerly known as Saltreia up to the 16th century, because of the transportation of salt through the area) lies between Huntingdon and Peterborough on the A1(M).

In the 1930s it was a quiet rural village with a population of about 500. After the Second World War the housing estates began to be built and altered Sawtry completely, from a straggling village to almost a town of over 5,000 people.

The village college (now a community college with a 6th form) was built in 1963. A new infant school was built in 1972 and a new junior school in 1982. The old school was bought by the Parish Council for use as a village hall.

As the village has developed so have the amenities. The sports facilities include a flourishing bowls club and football pitches with a clubhouse in Greenfields. The new Sawtry Sports Centre was opened in 1994 by the former Prime Minister John Major. It is situated within the college complex and offers a wide variety of sports and a swimming pool.

One can take a short walk up St Judith's Hill and find oneself in Aversley Wood. In Greenfields to the north, a conservation lake has been constructed to attract wildlife.

The WI hall is used on Sundays for worship by the Roman Catholics and there is a Methodist and Anglican church. The elderly and others are cared for by Caresco (care and resource organisation) which was founded in 1982. There are also two public houses and a fire station, and the industrial estate, which is due to be expanded, offers local employment.

The shops have changed. There is no longer a butcher or a baker. The premises are now occupied by a betting shop and a vet – a sign of the changing times?

❧ SHEPRETH

Shepreth is an attractive village of about 250 houses, lying eight miles south of Cambridge, next to the A10. The small river Shep makes an attractive feature as it wanders through the parish, to the delight of the fishing-inclined children. The younger children enjoy feeding the ducks. The southern parish boundary runs along Guilden Brook, which, like the river Shep runs into the river Cam.

Earlier inhabitants of Shepreth must have been energetic and enjoyed visiting neighbours as they established footpaths to all the nearby villages! These offer pleasant walks, often near the rivers. One runs from opposite the Green Man at the top of Frog End (beyond the bypass) up the 'Nave', along the river to the Fowlmere RSPB Reserve. A nave is the square in the centre of a cartwheel, and that was the size of pipe that was used to divert water from the river Shep along a ditch which ran past the houses in Frog End and can still be seen most of the way. This used to supply the cottages with water for all their needs except drinking; that had to be fetched from one of the three village pumps. The nearest pump has had to be moved to make room for the bypass.

The cottages on the north side of Frog End Road (which used to be over-run with frogs which reputedly sang as sweetly as larks in the night air in summer!) are mostly built end-on to the road as the land was divided into narrow strips following the Enclosure Act in 1823. The pattern of these can still be seen, although it is beginning to change as some of the back land is sold.

The village has a rich variety of houses, the small new groups blending happily with the traditional lath and plaster timber-framed houses so typical of Cambridgeshire. Roofs are varied and may be of thatch, tile or slate. Two mills which used to grind corn, powered by the Shep when it had a bigger flow of water, have been converted to houses.

The church, in a beautifully kept churchyard, is tucked away at

The Plough, Shepreth

the end of the High Street. It dates from Norman times with most of the following centuries leaving their mark. Local clunch and flint have been used in its walls as well as bricks, stone and cement.

If you turn into the village from the A10 through a beautiful avenue of beech trees, you can see one of the large pits, now filled with water. The pits were dug to provide chalk for use in the making of cement. The East Anglian Cement Company pit down Angle Lane provided a specialised cement that matched old mortar and was made specifically for the repair of old buildings, especially churches, including St Paul's Cathedral in London.

SOHAM

Until the draining of the fens a huge mere existed between Soham and Ely, the local people relying largely on fishing for their food and income. King Canute is known to have crossed the mere en route for the monastic establishment at Ely.

The present day Soham has a population of about 8,500 at the last count and still growing, and it is situated midway between Ely and Newmarket and approximately 20 miles from Cambridge. At first sight it might be thought that there is little of interest in Soham but closer investigation reveals a wealth of old houses, some dating back before the 17th century. On one old inn, now a house, can still be seen the painted sign 'Licensed to let a horse and gig'.

The history of Soham goes back to at least the Bronze and Iron Ages. Aerial photography and digs have revealed evidence of occupation during these periods. Whilst there is little sign of Roman occupation some artefacts of the period have been found. Of the Anglo-Saxon time a little more is known. Three cemeteries have been traced – one in the centre of Soham and two others on the Fordham side. In about AD 650 a monastery was founded in Soham by St Felix but it was sacked by the Danes in AD 870 and never rebuilt. This predates Ely Cathedral. In the fine parish church of St Andrew, traces of a painting on the north chancel wall are thought to be of St Felix in his vestments.

The present church dates back to the 12th century and amongst some of its interesting features are a beautiful hammerbeam roof with carved figures, carved poppy ends to some of the old benches, a fine transitional Norman arch and good examples of fairly modern stained glass including one window dedicated to William Case Morris, an Ely man educated in Soham who later became the 'Dr Barnardo' of Argentina. The tower contains a peal of ten bells which is well known to ringers throughout Cambridgeshire and much further afield. Outside the north porch is an interesting tomb commemorating Mary D'Aye, the great grand-daughter of Oliver Cromwell, who is buried in the cemetery.

Opposite the main entrance to the church is the 500 year old Fountain Inn which in former times was used for Court purposes and meetings of the local Justices. Although much of the public house was destroyed by fire in 1900, part of a panelled room, complete with a shield and coat of arms of Roger de Torel, dated 1533, still forms part of the present public lounge. Outside the inn, overhanging the road, is one of only two or three steelyards left in the country. This one is 300–400 years old and was used for weighing agricultural produce from pounds in weight to tons.

On 2nd June 1944 Soham was almost destroyed when an ammunition train caught fire but the town was saved by the bravery of Fireman J.W. Nightall GC (killed) and Driver B. Gimbert GC (badly injured), who detached the blazing wagon, and also the devotion to duty of Signalman F. Bridges (killed) and Guard H. Clarke who was severely shocked. Fireman Nightall, Driver Gimbert and Signalman Bridges all have roads in the town named after them. The medal of Mr Nightall is on display at the college.

Soham is unique in still having three commons, Quay Fen Common, East End Common and Angle Common.

At the present time Soham is a thriving community. Although individual farm owners still play a big part in the local economy there are also a number of large firms in the district. Added to this are two industrial estates where a wide variety of items are made which help to contribute to the wealth and employment of the district. Many local firms contributed to the setting up of the Soham and District Sports Centre which is now self supporting and extensively used by people of all ages.

🍁 SOMERSHAM

This large village standing on the Greenwich Meridian is situated on the edge of the fens. It was once a mainly fruit growing area. The village has expanded over recent years, and many of its inhabitants are commuters.

Somersham was recorded in the Domesday Book in 1086 and may have been visited by Hereward the Wake when fleeing from the Normans.

The parish church is said to stand on the remains of a 7th century wooden church that was built when the Kingdom of Mercia became Christian following the death of Penda.

During the 18th century the Somersham Spa waters were famous for health giving properties. In 1815 there was a terrible fire that destroyed much of the village of that time.

Today the ever-growing population is well provided for day-to-day, with a number of shops meeting basic needs. There are also schools, three churches, two health centres, four public houses and a library. Many organisations exist for all ages, interests and sporting activities, including a day centre for the elderly, which meets at the Victory Hall. The village proudly boasts of its Town Band, and the privately owned local museum.

In all a very active and caring community.

🍁 STANGROUND

At the beginning of the 20th century, Stanground consisted of four streets and several yards of three or four houses. Near the church stood the infants school and the senior school was situated in Chapel Street. Prior to this, school was held in the parish hall. There were two chapels, the Baptist and the Methodist, though the latter closed down some years ago. The village once boasted a number of shops including three bakers and six public houses, the oldest being the Blue Bell built in the 1700s and now a private residence. Three milkmen were on hand who delivered milk from their own cows twice a day to the villagers and a police station, blacksmith's and two builders could also be found here.

Stanground is now a much bigger place with housing estates, new schools and a college. A recent addition is the new community centre which was opened by the mayor and a long standing resident of the village, Annie Mills.

🍁 STAPLEFORD

Stapleford's village sign, which was erected to commemorate Elizabeth II's Silver Jubilee, depicts among other things, the stapol or white post which marked the ford across the nearby river Granta.

Some of the older buildings in Stapleford include Stapleford Hall, a large thatched 17th century building, and, at the other end of the social scale, Dormer Cottage, a small house dating back 300 years. Middlefield House, designed by Lutyens and built in 1908, is a notable example of a later style of architecture. The Slaughter-house, a small thatched building dating back to c1840, was originally the property of Mr Barker, a butcher in Stapleford. Next to it stand two attractive cottages restored by the Cambridgeshire Cottage Improvement Society in 1977.

St Andrew's church has been considerably altered and extended over the centuries, but its oldest surviving part is the Norman chancel arch. There is evidence of church bells in 1524 when 60 lambs were bequeathed to pay for a frame for them. All five bells were restored in 1911 and a sixth one added. Improvements to the church continue all the time. Substantial internal reorganisation, including the building of a new organ, took place in the 1980s.

One vicar, William Lee (died 1617), gave his house and land at Stapleford to the church and the poor. He is commemorated in a brass in the church. Another incumbent was Rev C.H.T.W. Daw, who died in 1897 and stated in his will that his right leg was to be sawn off by two surgeons so that he could fit into an ordinary sized coffin! A certificate was to be signed by the surgeons to the effect that they had carried out the work and they were to be paid three guineas each or take the limb in part payment if they so desired.

Stapleford Community School is still a thriving centre for community life in the village. It was opened in 1878 and the original red brick building still forms part of the present school, although it has been extended to many times its original size. The former schoolhouse was converted to a hostel for pupils of the adjacent Green Hedges School for handicapped children. This school and its pupils are taken very much to heart by the people of Stapleford and receive constant generous help and support from them.

Stapleford is twinned with Villedômer in the Loire valley. Every spring the villagers of Stapleford and Villedômer exchange visits, taking it in turn in alternate years to act as hosts. In July the teenagers exchange visits. They spend a week with their hosts, whereas the adults only manage a long weekend. Over the last fifteen years many firm friendships have developed and all twinners have a liking for Vouvray, the wine of the Loire.

The parish of Stapleford includes Wandlebury ring, a hill fort dating back to the 3rd century BC. Formerly the property of the Dukes of Leeds, Wandlebury is now a nature reserve and as such has many visitors from all over the county who enjoy walks, bird

Stapleford village sign

199

watching or simply sitting in the sun. The Godolphin Arabian, one of the three horses from which all British racing stock is descended, is buried at Wandlebury.

In 1989, the Magog Trust bought 163.5 acres of previously intensively farmed arable land on the Gog Magog hills in the north of the village, off the A1307 Cambridge to Linton road. The land is open freely to all for informal recreation and is an area for conservation. With a large car park it has two meadows sown with wild flowers and grasses native to chalk grassland and six woods, planted between 1990 and 1992, comprising 24,000 trees native to the chalk meadows of over a century ago. Two woods – Memorial and Magog – comprise trees planted in commemoration. It has a 2.5 mile fenced off-lead perimeter dog walk and is seeing the return of ground nestling birds like the lark and native flowering plants like the cowslip.

❦ STEEPLE MORDEN

There is a strongly held belief that Steeple Morden was originally South Morden and acquired its present day first name when the steeple was built to replace the tower which fell down in 1625. On the other hand 'Steeple' may well be a corruption of 'Staple', the name of a family who once lived in the village and whose coat of arms was in the church.

When the tower crashed down, causing considerable damage to the chancel, there were wrangles about who should do what work. And so runs the old jungle 'Steeple Morden silly people, Sold the bells to build a steeple' and for many generations people believed this. It is known that in 1742 the vicar and churchwardens applied for a faculty to sell two bells of the three and were doubtless successful, since there is now only one bell. The church of St Peter and St Paul was built in the 13th century to replace, possibly, a wooden one on the same site.

The Methodist church in Cheyney Street, known in the village as the Chapel, was built in 1875 on land given by Mr Strickland who lived in Victoria House, Hay Street.

More than 100 years ago the first school in the village – a dame school – was started in a cottage by The Cross; it was a 'plaiting school', the straw plaits being sent to Luton for the making of hats. The oldest part of the present school was built in 1865, an austere building, dimly lit and poorly heated, but over the years there have been vast improvements. There was a fall in numbers of pupils when in 1953 the older children left to go to Bassingbourn Village College, only to rise again in 1982 when Litlington primary school closed and the children were bussed from there to Steeple Morden. Extensions were made to the school to accommodate these children. At the present time there are 195 pupils at the school and in March 1998 further extensions were opened and dedicated by the Bishop of Huntingdon.

Steeple Morden is proud of its recreation ground and an excellent bowling green and club. Except for the post office situated at Prothero's Garage, which has operated since 1986, there are now no shops in the village. The general store in Hay Street which was also the post office until 1946 closed altogether in the spring of 1989. Prothero's Garage stopped serving petrol in 1996.

As with other villages in the area, Steeple Morden enjoyed prosperity from digging coprolites and in common with other villages there was a large number of public houses. There are now 2½ remaining in the village – the half comes from the Horse and Groom on the A505, half of which is in the parish of Litlington and the other half in Steeple Morden. The Jester at Odsey is actually in the parish of Steeple Morden and there is the Waggon and Horses opposite the church. The last public house to close its doors in the village was the Fox in 1973.

History has it that ghosts and murders have been known in the village. It is believed that a packman visiting the village hawking his goods was seen to make his way to a farmhouse for the night but was

201

never seen again. Historian Andrew Pye believes that this was not the only murder; he believes that Abraham Cambers of Shingay Road was shot dead by his nephew in 1875, which made history because the murderer was the first to be reprieved from the death sentence.

Many years later the village was unique because, despite a number of men being called up during the Second World War and serving on most battle fronts, all returned safely and so no new names were added to the war memorial.

In 1939 land being farmed by the Jarman family and some by the late Graham Parish on the Litlington road was requisitioned for an airfield, first used as an RAF training field and later used by the Americans of the 355th Fighter Group. No story about Steeple Morden would be complete without a mention of these young American fighter pilots who dubbed the village 'home from home' because of the hospitality they received in those dark days and whom those who survived have never forgotten. Members of the 355th Fighter Memorial Association continue to keep in touch with the village, returning for reunions from time to time. The memorial on the Litlington road is a constant reminder to Steeple Morden of the wartime days and the Americans never forget the village either. They have generously contributed to the purchase of books for the use of the village primary school.

In 1952 the village hall – a Nissen hut – was presented to the village by the late Mr Ernie Pepper and officially opened by his daughter. As Mrs Cynthia Clayton she performed a similar ceremony in 1973 when the present village hall was officially opened.

🍁 STETCHWORTH

Stetchworth lies between Newmarket and Cambridge. The Devil's Dyke runs very close to the village, which has existed as a village since the 11th century. It presently has a population of about 600.

Formerly the inhabitants of Stetchworth were employed in

agriculture and in providing local services. Nowadays they work in Cambridge and elsewhere, although stud farms still provide employment on the land. The National Stud lies within Stetchworth's boundaries and other local stud farms are the Egerton Stud, the Collin Stud and the Stetchworth Park Stud. The Marquis of Granby is the only remaining public house; the Live and Let Live, which served as a hotel for several years, is now a private house, as is the former White Horse Hotel. There is still a post office, albeit part-time. Several travelling shops visit the village.

A part-time general store run by volunteers is housed in the Ellesmere Centre, a multi-purpose building opened in 1984 to extend and complement the Ellesmere Hall. The new building provides sports facilities and accommodation for many clubs and classes. It was designed for use by the parishes of Stetchworth, Woodditton, Dullingham, Kirtling, Westley Waterless, Brinkley and Burrough Green. It is one of only three such centres in the country, set up by the Development Commission to improve the standard of rural life.

Lord Gorges, the Superintendent and Surveyor General of the corporation which drained the Great or Bedford level, lived in Stetchworth and in the north aisle of the nave of Stetchworth church there is a large monument to Henry, his son, who died in 1674 aged 19.

Graffiti are not new. Two pillars in the north side of the nave have medieval figures scratched on them. Thought to have been drawn to record a visit to Stetchworth by Queen Philippa, they depict a woman wearing an elaborate headdress of gold wire, an owl with a similar headdress, a man, a cat and a type of wader bird – a common sight before the fens were drained.

Mill Lane found fame in 1981 when a young family discovered treasure buried beneath their pantry floor. They found gold sovereigns and half sovereigns with a face value of £100, valued today at £40,000, dating from 1818–1825. A treasure trove enquiry was held but the coins were returned to the finders.

People say that, because of the high incidence of disease, Stetchworth was one of the first villages locally to be connected to the mains sewer. The need for an efficient sewer may have given rise to Dullingham's epithet for the village – 'stinking Stetchworth'. The Alley, a narrow lane off the High Street, was formerly known more colourfully as 'Turd Alley' for at the end of the Alley villagers without modern sanitation used to empty the buckets from their privies!

🍁 STIBBINGTON & WANSFORD

The village of Stibbington was originally part of the Roman town of Durobrivae, and there are still Roman kilns in the corner of the field by a small council estate called Roman Drive. The village meandered along the Great North Road, the boundary being the river Nene. A lane passes by the church of St John the Baptist to the river, and there used to be a ford across to the village of Sutton. The river was the ecclesiastical boundary between the villages of Stibbington and Wansford until 1976, when the lower portion was joined to Wansford for ecclesiastical purposes only. The jurisdiction of the Stibbington Parish Council however, still remains to halfway across the bridge. The village of Stibbington was completely bisected by the dual carriageway of the A1 when it was built and the part which contains the Haycock and the local shops is now commonly and erroneously known as Wansford.

The village of Stibbington formerly had the services of the following: two bakeries, a blacksmith, two wheelwrights, a saddler, a tailor, a stationer, a butcher, a post office, three grocery shops and two schools. One of these was the Wansford School for Young Ladies, which was situated at Barnaby House. Now there remains only a grocery cum post office, a shoe shop and a dress shop.

The Haycock Hotel was a famous coaching inn and parts of the present building are thought to date back to the 13th century. It was originally called the Swan but was renamed the Haycock in the 18th century. Post horses were kept here for travellers journeying on the Great North Road and Queen Victoria spent the night at this hotel two years before she ascended the throne.

During the 18th and early 19th centuries, Wansford had a paper making industry which was situated in the grounds now known as Stibbington House. The only reminder today of the paper making mills is a public house called the Paper Mills.

Wansford's church, dedicated to St Mary, and part of which was built in Saxon times, stands on a hill looking down over the slowly meandering river Nene.

There has been a crossing over the river probably since the Domesday Book was compiled. In 1571, three arches of the wooden bridge were destroyed in a flood. Wansford has three bridges. The oldest bridge was built in the 16th century and links the village of Wansford with the parish of Stibbington. The second and third bridges were built across the river near the Mermaid Inn, now a Little Chef, about 1975 when the A1 was developed into a dual carriageway.

Wansford was once important as a river port and has interesting old associations. Less than a century ago, a quaint old flagstone quay presented a busy sight, where cargoes of coal, wheat and other grain were loaded and unloaded.

The river is a popular haunt for anglers. Walking along the river in summer, you'll find a number of leisure craft berthed by the old bridge. The worst flooding within living memory occurred on 12th April 1998. The rising of the Nene caused flooding in many properties and extensive water damage.

A nearby attraction is the Nene Valley Railway, which is run by a Steam Preservation Society and is a standard gauge steam railway, running from Wansford Station in Stibbington to Peterborough NVR Station, via Ferry Meadows and Orton Mere.

🍁 STILTON

Nearly 2,000 years ago the Roman legions marched along Ermine Street on the road that was later to become one of Britain's busiest thoroughfares – the Great North Road.

Two hundred and fifty years ago, travellers were still using the same route, stopping at the many posting houses in the village. One traveller, Lord Harley, is reputed to have stopped at the Bell Inn, which was already over 200 years old, and sampled the unusual cheese said to have been made in Stilton. He was not impressed! Nevertheless Stilton cheese, although no longer made in the area, continues to be one of the country's most popular cheeses and is often called 'The King of English cheese'.

Today, the travellers are replaced by tourists trying to find the 'cheese factory'. Though unsuccessful in this, their visits are not in vain, for the ancient Bell and Angel still stand picturesquely commanding the village centre, with its ancient pump. Not far away stands the church of St Mary Magdalene, with its 13th century nave arcades and 15th century font.

To the north is Norman Cross, where the old mail coaches from Peterborough and Lincoln joined the Great North Road. This is also the site of the Norman Cross prisoner-of-war camp, where French and Dutch prisoners were housed during the Napoleonic Wars. All that remains of this period is a large white house – the former Governor's residence.

Nearby, on the side of the A1, is a column surmounted by a spread eagle, a memorial to 1,770 French soldiers who died whilst in captivity. Ironically the memorial was unveiled in July 1914, just a few days before the 'war to end all wars' began.

Not all the prisoners returned to their homeland at the end of the Napoleonic Wars as can be seen by the many Anglicized French names found amongst the local population.

A different kind of 'invasion' followed in the 1940s, when

American servicemen came to operate from the many wartime airfields that criss-crossed East Anglia. 'Yanks' were billeted at Stilton and an elderly inhabitant remembers village housewives taking in 'American washing' and several young ladies leaving as GI brides.

There is an annual event, known as 'Cheese Rolling'. In this keenly contested race, teams from all the surrounding area, many in fancy dress, bowl a 'cheese' (a large log sawn from a telegraph pole and painted to look like a Stilton cheese) along the High Street. The winning team is awarded a crate of beer and a whole Stilton cheese. The street is lined with stalls, increasing the fair-like atmosphere whilst, at the same time, raising money for charity.

🍁 STOW CUM QUY

Originally two settlements, Stow and Quy were regarded as one village as early as the 1086 Domesday Book. Locally it is known as Quy (but never as Stow).

Stow means a 'holy place' and, although only some 17 metres above sea level, it stands up above the surrounding fenland. It is thought that the Saxon church built here was on an earlier pagan site. A fragment of a 12th century arch can be seen in the present church, rebuilt in 1340, which stands on the edge of the village next to the busy Quy interchange on the Cambridge bypass. The Rev Richard Minter who died aged 91 in 1997, after 50 years' ministry in Quy, was the last Vicar of Quy. Now Bottisham, Lode and Quy share the same vicar.

Stow Manor, long since disappeared, was inhabited by the D'Engayne family until 1367. The last 'Lady Gains' perhaps desolate at having no children, is said still to walk the river bank, hung about with chains, beckoning and promising to show any who dare to follow where she has buried treasure.

Quy comes from the Anglo-Saxon words for 'Cow Isle' but 'we'ew whully lazy hereabouts and now tha's jest plain Quy'. Quy also had its own church, St Nicholas, near the crossroads in the centre of the village. Evidently it had been in ruins for so long that the story grew up that Quy people wanted a church but as fast as they built up the walls the Devil came and pulled them down again overnight so that Quy did not get a church.

Quy Hall belonged to the Martin family, the London bankers, from 1720 to 1854. Clement Francis, a Cambridge solicitor with a large family, bought the property in 1854 and the house was partly rebuilt and restored to its earlier appearance by the London architect W. White in 1868–1870. The Francis family still own Quy estate. At the end of the last war they owned 70% of the houses in Quy; since then there have been council and private houses built and some of the older properties have been sold though some 25% of the housing is still part of the estate.

Quy Hall drawn by Jim Watts

In February the shrubbery, the island in the grounds of Quy Hall and the surrounding woodlands are a carpet of white snowdrops and golden aconites amidst the dark green ivy leaves. During the First World War, the Francis family allowed the snowdrops to be picked and the bunches were sent by train to London to raise money for the Red Cross. The custom of snowdrop picking has been allowed to continue to this day when a gallant band of ladies brave the icy winds picking bunches for sale to Cambridge florists for church funds.

The village has a population just under 500 but it boasts three pubs and a hotel, all of which serve good meals! There is a shop-cum-post office and a garage. Alas, the village school closed in 1978 and children of all ages now go to Bottisham for their education. Most people commute to Cambridge which is only five miles away, but there is a small industrial site in the centre of the village.

At the southern edge of the village are 70 acres of Quy Fen over which Quy, Horningsea and Fen Ditton have equal rights. Now the fen is let for grazing and the income shared by the villages. In olden times all parishioners had the right to cut hay or peasticks, but no animals were allowed to graze there. There is a memorial stone to William Ison, aged 29, who was struck by lightning when cutting hay in 1873. In the late 1880s Mrs Francis, as lady of the manor, gave permission for coprolites to be dug in Quy Fen in order to provide work for local people. Work was carried on for about four years but the company was wound up in debt and the last of the 'cuts' were left to fill with water instead of being filled in. The largest cut in Quy Fen has since then always been popular with swimmers, though tragically at least two people have been drowned there. The area round the cut has rare fen plants, is a breeding ground for dragonflies and damselflies and has thus been designated a Site of Special Scientific Interest. It can only be visited by foot as cars are not allowed on the droveways leading to Quy Fen.

🍁 STOW LONGA

Stow Longa, west of Huntingdon, has 55 houses and 130 people. Over the centuries the population has fluctuated, reaching a high of 188 in 1841. There are no pubs, no school, no shop. Kimbolton is only two miles away. The community has a farming tradition, growing mainly cereal crops and sheep!

The church, St Botolph's, dates from the 13th century. The tower is the highest point in the old Huntingdonshire at 61 metres (200 ft) above sea level. The church originally had three bells but there is only one now; the other two were last spotted in Kimbolton in the 1920s. The church was very important in the 13th century and there is the nationally famous Beckoning Mermaid Priest's Door.

During the Second World War an airfield was constructed on the hill to the south of the village. This was used extensively by the 379th Bombardment Group of the Eighth American Air Force between May 1943 and July 1945. Some 330 combat missions flew from here in B-17 bombers.

On the outskirts of the village is Station Master's Cottage, first mentioned in the 1871 census. The cottage sits along the line of the railway from Huntingdon to Kettering. There was no station here, merely a halt or siding.

🍁 STRETHAM

Stretham, meaning 'Home on the Street', takes its name from the Roman road Akeman Street (now the A10). The high ground on which this fen village stands has been occupied since prehistoric times.

The focal point of the village is a fine 15th century stone cross that, unlike those in neighbouring villages, escaped destruction by Henry VIII's vandals. St James's church, with its beautiful old stone spire, stands nearby, and also the Red Lion pub and restaurant and the much valued post office and general stores.

A network of well-kept footpaths surrounds the village and a walk along the Old West river takes you to Stretham Old Engine, built in the 1830s. Its 30 ft waterwheel, driven by steam, lifted 30 tons of water at a turn, out of the low fen drains and into the higher river. You can imagine the size of the machinery needed for this task! It is all still there, beautifully preserved and well worth a visit. The other reminder of a bygone industry is the high, handsome black Tower Windmill that stands at the north end of the High Street and looks across the countryside to where Ely Cathedral floats in majesty on the fens.

Stretham is proud of its history but it has its feet planted firmly in the present. The primary school has doubled in size and there is a flourishing preschool playgroup and the all day Windmill Nursery. There are up-to-date sports facilities and a variety of clubs for all age groups, as well as a good bus service. Agriculture has been the premier industry here for centuries, but the Old Village School houses Studio Audio, creators of a world leading disk editing device.

The most recent development in the village is a home for autistic adults in the Old Rectory (now Juniper House). This magnificent old building, spanning six centuries, has been meticulously restored and equipped and given a new lease of life to take it far into the new millennium.

🍁 STUNTNEY

Stuntney is a tiny place now but in the past it has had a place in history. When Hereward the Wake was defending Ely against the Normans, Stuntney was one of the bridgeheads of the Norman attack. A few hundred years later Stuntney laid another claim to fame as the home of Oliver Cromwell's mother, one of the Steward family, at the little Elizabethan manor – Stuntney Hall – which stood on Hall Hill. Steward Close is named after the family.

The most important and probably the oldest building in Stuntney is the church of the Holy Cross, with its Saxon origins. It has two well preserved chevron arches, one around the entrance door on the south side and another inside the church, and these are good examples of Norman architecture.

Visitors to the village today notice the beautiful village sign with its shire horse, which was made for the village by local craftsmen. Stuntney has a long association with the shire horse. Before the advent of the steam traction engine and the tractor, the horse was the most important source of power on the land at Cole Ambrose Farm in Stuntney and around the turn of the century there were about 200 horses, shires and hackneys, on the farm. Cole Ambrose was the founder member of the Shire Horse Society and one of the leading breeders in the country.

These horses can still be seen in the village today although they are no longer worked. They are the responsibility of Mr 'Dekker' Murfitt.

The village 'pound' was an important feature during the days when many farm animals or horses strayed from their owners, and were kept in the pound until they were claimed. The keeper of the pound was obliged to receive any animals offered into his custody. Today the pound forms part of the property Anchor House, once a public house and now a charming private house.

The most macabre relic of all was probably the tomb which was found by men sub-soiling the land at Thorney Hill. The tomb contained a skeleton which was taken to Ely Museum where it can still be seen today.

Although many features of village life have disappeared, there is one old custom which has been revived and that is the ancient ceremony of 'beating the bounds' which takes place at Rogationtide just before Ascension Day. A procession from the church headed by the priest, a server bearing a crucifix and parishioners carrying willow wands, stop at various well-known points along the parish boundary to beat the bounds. Hymns are sung and prayers said to ask for a good harvest. Although Stuntney is a tiny village the boundary is very extensive so nowadays stopping points are limited, and the opportunity is taken to combine this ceremony with a picnic outing.

🍁 SUTTON (NEAR ELY)

This village is but one of some 60 Suttons in England, and one of at least four in the fens! Its full name is Sutton in the Isle, being located on one of the natural islands of the fens. The first inhabitants are unknown; however, Neolithic flint tools have been found and the tooth of the woolly mammoth was found in the garden of a house in the High Street, and was used for a number of years as a door stop! The earliest recorded reference to the village dates from AD 673, when Etheldreda, daughter of King Anna of East Anglia, sought peace in Sutton, although the island on which it stood was overrun by the Danes in AD 870.

In the Domesday Book, the village name was shown as Sudtone, however by 1170 it had changed to Suth and in 1246 to Suttone. In 1086 the population is recorded as being 9 sokemen (freemen), 8 villeins (villagers) each with 7½ acres, 15 cotter (cottagers) and 7 serfs (labourers) and there was a small wood which provided sustenance for 5 pigs. The total village was valued at £12.

During the 16th century the parish was known locally as 'Golden Sutton', from its abundant rich cherry orchards, vineyards and wealth of sheep.

The construction of the present parish church, St Andrew's, was commenced in 1350, but the roll of vicars is traceable back to 1170, with a vicarage being established in 1254. Standing on high ground its unique tower, known locally as the 'Pepperpot', can be seen for miles around. It contains six bells, inscribed with dates between 1654 and 1819. The stained glass east window is Victorian, with an outstanding modern (1975) stained glass window by Laurence Lee

213

on the south side of the chancel. The font is 15th century, with a four petalled flower design. Opposite the church stood the old Guild Hall, with Guild Chaplains recorded from the beginning of the 15th century.

Dating from the 14th century is the Burystead Farm, which is a two-storey chapel, built by the Prior and Convent of Ely, with additions made in 1742. The monks of Ely employed a Lay Bailiff to be responsible for their manor and he lived at the Burystead. Within the ground there are numerous graves.

A schoolmaster, William Heye, was licensed in 1579, and in 1798 boys were being taught in a room in the church under the belfry. The present school was built in 1860, for £853, following the amalgamation of the four existing schools under the National Schools Society. By 1863 the school roll was 200 children. The last village dame school closed in 1892, and application to extend the school to accommodate 285 children was made. This extension was built in 1912, with further additions made in 1968 and 1976, with a major reconstruction in 1991.

John Wesley visited Sutton in November 1774, staying two nights and preaching in a large barn. Wesley recorded in his diary that it was well filled and at subsequent meetings the attendance increased. A Wesleyan Methodist congregation was established in 1790, with the chapel being rebuilt in 1914. A Primitive Methodist chapel was established in 1880, closing in 1935. The Particular Baptist chapel was built in 1791, enlarged in 1820 with a gallery added in 1844.

The Romans were the first to attempt to drain the fens, by embanking the fen and clearing woodlands, so as to introduce arable farming. Following their departure and the arrival of the Saxons, the drainage dykes fell into misuse and neglect, with the fens flooding again. In 1650 Oliver Cromwell commissioned Vermuyden to construct the New Bedford river; this was completed within two years. However, by 1680 the peat fen land had begun to shrink, and flooding again became a problem. In 1696 the north bank gave way at Sutton Gault leaving a gap 60 feet wide. Not until the introduction of windmills to pump the water from the lower lying land into the river was the fen successfully drained. Nature still continues to challenge these man-made rivers, and flooding can still occur, with the last such flood in 1947; all the riverbanks were reconstructed again during 1993.

The wartime aerodrome in Sutton parish was named after neighbouring Mepal, to avoid confusion with the other Suttons. From June 1943 this was home to 75 (NZ) Squadron, whose Maori motto was 'Ake ake Kia Kaka' (For ever and ever be strong), one of the most famous squadrons in Bomber Command. The airfield finally closed in 1963 and is now a business park.

🍁 SUTTON (NEAR PETERBOROUGH)

Sutton, a village situated half a mile south of the A47, between Wansford and Castor, has 46 houses and all but four of the original cottages have been modernised.

The manor house of Sutton is The Grange, built in the 17th century. It was owned by the Ecclesiastical Commissioners and sold by them to the Rev Hopkinson in 1898. The church, dedicated to St Michael and All Angels, was originally dedicated to St Giles, the patron saint of cripples, lepers and nursing mothers. It was built early in the 12th century and only the chancel arch supports survive, but much 13th century work remains. The church was largely rebuilt in 1867–8 out of the proceeds of the sale of land at Sutton Heath for the building of the Wansford branch railway.

West of the church, the road has become an overgrown muddy track to the river Nene. There was a ford across to Stibbington, but it was unused for some time and it was finally destroyed by dredging in the 1950s to permit river traffic.

The farm, Manor Farm, is 17th century, and the 18th century cottage opposite was originally the Cross Keys public house.

Sutton village is now a designated conservation area. The site of

215

the old Roman road Ermine Street, which ran from London to Lincoln, is to the east of the village at the site of the Sutton Cross, which is the junction point of the parish boundaries of Sutton, Upton and Ailsworth.

🍁 SWAFFHAM BULBECK

Swaffham Bulbeck and its hamlet Commercial End are situated at the head of an artificial waterway or 'lode' approximately seven miles north east of Cambridge.

There are several interesting buildings still intact. Burgh Hall, once one of three manors, is a richly timbered 'Wealden style' house, now a farm. Lordship Cottage is identified as a 13th century one cell chapel, with Tudor additions. The 'Abbey' was founded in the late 12th century by Isobel de Bolebec as a Benedictine priory for nuns. Never a rich foundation, it was surrendered by the last prioress, Joan Spilman, at the Dissolution of the Monasteries in 1536. It is reputed that she liked the neighbourhood so much that she remained in a cave in the vicarage garden for at least a year afterwards. Today, the vaulted undercroft is all that remains, with an 18th century home built above it.

The church of St Mary is mainly 14th century with an earlier tower. There are some interesting carved bench ends within.

The Rev Leonard Jenyns (1828–1849) was perhaps the most notable vicar of the village. An ardent botanist, he was proposed as botanist to accompany Captain Fitzroy on the *Beagle* but refused and proposed instead his friend Charles Darwin.

There is also a Free Church in Commercial End. The Free Church Society was formed in 1899 and their first chapel was known as 'The Tin Tabernacle'. An appeal was launched for funds for a permanent chapel which was finally opened in 1926.

Although farming was a dominant feature, the village was not entirely reliant on it. The fen itself had provided peat cutting and reed cutting. Saffron had been grown reasonably successfully during the 16th and 17th centuries. With the draining of the fen during the late 17th century a navigable route was opened to Commercial End (or Newnham as it was known). Wharves were built and a trading establishment began which reached its peak in the early 19th century under Thomas Bowyer – sending out agricultural produce and importing coal and wines etc. The water trade was eventually killed by the railway, but the unique appearance of Commercial End today is the legacy that Bowyer left.

Village life has changed much since then. In 1851 the population supported three shopkeepers, two shoemakers, two cornmillers, three carpenters, two wheelwrights, a harnessmaker, bricklayers and shepherds as well as five public houses plus other beer sellers. Today there is only one public house, as the Royal Oak was closed in 1989, and a shop-cum-post office. During the 1990s farmers converted their redundant old timbered barns and some are now occupied by 'new high tech' companies.

Education in the village came via two gifts of money in 1710 and 1722 to found a charity school for the poor children. The new National School opened in 1874 is still in use today and being enlarged with extra school rooms.

All was not hard work. At the beginning of the 20th century a wife sale was recorded as taking place at the Royal Oak. Villagers were amused when two tinkers arrived, one of whom offered his wife for sale at auction. She was finally sold for half-a-crown to his companion!

These days the village supports a successful series of Gilbert and Sullivan operas in one of the old farm barns instead!

🍁 SWAFFHAM PRIOR & REACH

Swaffham Prior derives its name from the word 'Swaffham' meaning 'a homestead of the Swabians' – an ancient German tribe who were

Roman mercenaries – and 'Prior' referring to the fact that it once belonged to the Prior of Ely.

The village stands on a chalk ridge on one of the few hills in Cambridgeshire, five miles west of Newmarket. It is bounded by fenland on its western side and is longitudinal, as are most villages on the fen edge.

Two churches in the same churchyard stand above the curved main street, which is lined by a mixture of demure cottages and Georgian houses with shady gardens. There are several splendid old manor houses. The 10th century church, St Mary's, has a fine 13th century tower onto which a stainless steel spire with a crown was recently added. The second church, St Cyriac's and St Julitta's, was built a century later, for a separate parish. The two churches amalgamated in 1667 and both continued to function until St Mary's spire was struck by lightning in 1767 and the church was closed down for a time. However, it is St Mary's which is in use today, whilst St Cyriac's is used as a social centre and houses a fine set of bells.

Much of the limestone used in the churches comes from quarries in the neighbouring village of Reach, a small enclave in the parish of Swaffham Prior. It claims to be the oldest settlement in the district on the basis of Stone Age flints found there. The seven mile earthwork called Devil's Dyke starts at Reach. Excavations carried out in 1924 showed that it was built in the 8th century as an East Anglian defence against Mercia, to the west. Reach has a Royal Charter and a famous annual fair. Locals call it the Kingdom of Reach.

Following the Industrial Revolution and the mechanisation of farms the population of Swaffham Prior has decreased considerably, to just over 700. There is now only one public house, no village shop or post office and few tradesmen call. All shopping has to be done in nearby towns. Most of the inhabitants these days are commuters. Despite the lack of amenities, there is a flourishing primary school, Baptist church and an excellent newly renovated village hall. There are also two fully restored windmills, one of which is in business. There are several clubs and a great community spirit fostered both by the old indigenous families and the newcomers who have been attracted into this lovely village.

🍁 SWAVESEY

Swavesey is a fen edge village, eight miles west of Cambridge. Its southern boundary extends one mile along the A14 and to the north, west and east, lie the villages of Over, Fen Drayton and Longstanton. At the north end of the village stands the parish church, St Andrew's, which is mainly of the 13th and 14th centuries although there is evidence of an earlier Saxon building in the present building. By the 19th century the church was in a dilapidated state and in 1867 extensive restoration work was carried out which has resulted in the beautiful church we have today.

Adjoining the church is the site of a priory, founded by Count Alan of Brittany. Earthworks still remain and aerial photographs show that the priory covered quite a large area. Near the church stands the manor house, a charming building, which in the 16th century belonged to the Cutts family.

As well as the priory and a castle, of which earthworks still remain, Swavesey was also a market town. A market and fair was granted by Henry III to Alan de la Zouch in 1244. It would seem that Swavesey developed into a thriving commercial centre with boats using the dock in Market Street. Although we have no records of when the market ceased to operate, the name Market Street still survives and remains of the dock were filled in during 1964.

A few very early houses have survived in Swavesey, the most notable one being at Ryders Farm, Middle Watch, which dates from 1280. This has recently been sympathetically restored.

In the early 1950s the population of Swavesey was approximately 1,000. During the next thirty years there was a steady increase, much of it taking place on the Whitton Close, Priory Avenue, Carters Way and Thistle Green estates. This increase in the population has integrated into the existing community well and Swavesey has retained a pleasant village atmosphere.

In 1993 Swavesey was designated a rural growth village where development of up to 400 houses in estates or small groups could take place, and in 1995 housing development in School Lane began, so again there is a steady rise in the population. Swavesey has been fortunate during the years to have retained a considerable amount of local employment. It is hoped that with the transfer of some of the employment from the Barwell industrial site to the new Buckingway Business Park near the A14, employment will increase and prevent Swavesey becoming a commuter village.

Despite the fact that the village has doubled in size over the last forty-five years it has, during that time, lost many of its village shops and tradesmen. In the early 1950s there were three grocers with rounds in the village, four butchers, three bakers delivering bread and cakes, and the daily newspaper was delivered every morning. There was a blacksmith shoeing local horses, a shoemaker working in his shop in the High Street and two carpenters' shops where men were employed making window frames, doors and ladders besides repairing anything made of wood. The railway station was a hive of activity on summer afternoons, when horse and trolley loads of fruit were being loaded into trucks before starting the journey to a city market.

The village college is continuing to expand and provides an excellent educational facility for children in Swavesey and the surrounding villages. The primary school provides an excellent start for village children and is an attraction to home buyers with children moving into the area. The goods station is now the headquarters of the popular MG Owners Club, and for recreation the Mere Fen nature reserve provides attractive walks for local ramblers and bird watchers and visitors to the village.

Swavesey has always been a friendly village in which to live and long may that continue.

🍁 THORNEY

Until 1910 Thorney village and the parish comprising over 40,000 acres was included in the estate of the Duke of Bedford. He had received the area of Thorney as a gift from a grateful sovereign in recognition of the Duke's labours in draining the fens. After 1910 the estate was sold to the tenant farmers for, in many cases, as little as ten shillings an acre.

The incumbency of the Abbey remained in the gift of the Duke during the lifetime of the vicar, the Reverend W. Symons. As there were three other places where Anglican services were held it was necessary to have a curate. His stipend was the responsibility of the parishioners and to this end an annual tea and concert was held in the Abbey Rooms. The local farmers' wives brought their finest crockery and each catered for one table. They provided huge quantities of food to the great enjoyment of all!

Throughout the years of the close dependence on the Duke of Bedford and also after the dispersal of the estate, the people of Thorney had learnt to be self sufficient in many ways. Under the auspices of the Duke many craftsmen had flourished, including carpenters, wheelwrights, blacksmiths, millers, builders and bakers. When the farmers became landowners there entered into the whole community a sense of competition. Clubs were formed and cricket, football, bowls and tennis were played in season. A shire horse and foal show was held annually on the first Thursday in June and a Flower Show attracted a lot of support.

At that time there was a large acreage of grass and vast quantities of beef cattle and sheep were raised. Many horses and foals were reared in strong competition with neighbouring farmers. Some of these horses were commandeered by the Ministry of War for hauling guns to the battlefields in France during the First World War. One farmer exported some of his fine animals to the American state of Illinois where four brothers by the name of Truman carried on extensive farming. These men were related to a man of the same name who subsequently became President of the USA.

The majority of the grassland was put to the plough during the Second World War when the National War Effort demanded the maximum production of food. These solid countrymen rose to the occasion with unstinted zeal and helped to fill the nation's larder in an hour of desperate need.

🍁 THORNHAUGH

Thornhaugh village lies west of the A1, nine miles north west of Peterborough. Its name is derived from the Anglo Saxon and means a thorn enclosed low-lying meadow beside a stream. There is evidence of a settlement as far back as the 12th century and for many centuries, the population would have consisted of land owners, farmers, clergymen, millers and workers on the land, in the woods and quarries. Thornhaugh is a village with a small static population but the area within the parish is one of the largest in the county of Cambridgeshire. Nowadays there is no shop, no school, no public house or bus service within the village but it has great character and beauty to compensate for the lack of facilities. It was declared a conservation area in 1979.

St Andrew's church contains a monument to the memory of Sir William Russell, First Baron Russell of Thornhaugh. He is recorded as holding high office in the service of Queen Elizabeth I and was a comrade-in-arms and close friend of Sir Philip Sidney. Sir Philip bequeathed to Sir William Russell his suit of gilded armour and many people thought that the helmet which was displayed for many years above the monument in the church, was part of this armour. Although this was not so, the helmet was nevertheless found to be of great value and was promptly removed for safe keeping.

Sacrewell Mill, now part of Sacrewell Farm and Visitors' Centre, lies half a mile to the east of the Great North Road in the north east angle of the junction between the A1 and the A47. The mill stream forms the boundary between the parishes of Thornhaugh and Wansford. Sacrewell Mill, as it now stands, dates from about the middle of the 18th century; a stone in the north west corner of the main building bears the date 1755. It is likely, however, that the mill had several predecessors, as there are remains of three substantial Romano-British villas on Sacrewell Farm, showing evidence of grain drying and malting. It is thought that the Romans introduced the watermill.

Sacrewell is steeped in history and the farm probably derives its name from a very strong spring which rises in one of the fields. There have been many dwellers at Sacrewell for hundreds of years. Neolithic implements have been found and there are several prehistoric circles of uncertain date and use. In Roman times the farm probably supplied food for the industrial population based on Castor and Nene valley potteries. Weapons, tools of flint and Roman pottery are still found, which dates the buildings at about AD 300.

🍁 THRIPLOW

It is believed that Thriplow takes its name from Trippa (or Tryppa) 'low' or 'hill'. Thus you pronounce Thriplow as Triplow – the 'h' being added much later on. The word 'low' is frequently found in English place-names meaning a low hill or small mound. Early maps of the district show a 'tumulus' in the field behind Thriplow church. Archaeologists excavating the tumulus in the 1950s were able to date cremated remains to the Bronze Age and later Iron Age finds were also discovered.

In Saxon times Thriplow was the most important of the local villages and represented the Thriplow Hundred – an area comprising ten villages from Trumpington in the north to Fowlmere in the south. The Hundred Court met in Thriplow from time to time until the end of the 19th century.

The Smithy, Thriplow

Today there are about 400 inhabitants in the old Thriplow parish. The village boasts an award-winning public house called the Green Man, a village shop with a post office, a bus service to Cambridge, a cricket meadow, village green and recreation ground. The Church of England primary school was opened in 1863/4 with 45 pupils, rising to over 100 in 1900. After a period of low numbers of pupils, for a second time there are now 100+ pupils on the school roll.

Thriplow church is dedicated to St George and All Saints and is built of Barnack stone, flint and clunch. Although the current building dates from the Norman times there has been a church on the same site since about AD 900. Of particular interest are the Norman font, Norman pillars outside the north transept, the remains of narrow lancet windows in the chancel and the screen. In 1981 villagers undertook the task of providing new tapestry-covered kneelers for the church; some show pictures of village houses and others depict local groups and organisations.

Until 1743 there were four bells in the church and a fifth was added in that year. These lasted until 1995 when benefactors provided the means to strengthen the tower and to rehang the bells. A sixth bell was added and now the village boasts a local home-grown team of bellringers who ring regularly on Sundays and for special occasions such as Daffodil Weekend.

In 1963 the Daffodil Weekend was born with several private homes and gardens open to the public at the height of the daffodil-flowering season. Refreshments were provided in the school and elsewhere and the money raised from this event was shared between the school and the Church Restoration Fund. After the first four years when the festival had grown to include many village gardens and village helpers an independent Daffodil Committee took over the organisation.

Nowadays thousands of visitors swell the streets of Thriplow every Daffodil Weekend, enjoying the many aspects of village life – meeting and talking to residents, viewing the gardens, visiting the craft stalls and exhibitions, sampling the teas and home-made cakes at the refreshment points and watching the many demonstrations, whether they are working sheep dogs, heavy horses or the working smithy. Special entertainment is arranged for the children and a free mini-bus provides transport around the village.

All this is a far cry from the first two or three Daffodil Weekends but the spirit of those early days prevails with the money raised from each weekend being shared between village organisations, the church and the school as well as an external charity – a different one chosen each year. Currently, however, most of the profits are going towards the building of a new village hall ready for the Thriplovians of the 21st century.

🍁 TOFT

Toft is a small village approximately six miles to the west of Cambridge on the B1046 road. Although there is evidence of habitation going back to the Romans and earlier, we associate the village more with the Danes. The village began in the troubled days when the Danes and the English struggled for possession of Eastern England (around AD 750–950). It is reasonably thought that a Dane decided to settle here and set up his 'Toft', his homestead. By 1066 it was a settled community.

The Normans took over the lordship of the land in 1066 and after a number of slight changes the village was passed to the bishopric of Ely in 1109. It has been estimated that just under 200 people lived here at that time. At the top of the social structure were the 'tenants-in-chief' who held land direct from the king, two men who held 'knight's fees' and seven or eight 'spokesmen' but the majority were serfs, tied to the soil. At the bottom were a few slaves.

It is not known when the first church was built but there is certain knowledge that one was here in 1278, very probably built of wood. It was rebuilt in stone when John de Merton was rector (1349–1354). One gets the impression that it developed into a very beautiful church with stained glass windows and brass memorials. After the execution of Charles I (1649) the reforming Bishop of Ely sent William Dowsing to root out objects of superstition. There followed great destruction.

Among these objects is listed a bell with the inscription 'Orate pro anima Sanctae Katherinae', for destroying which Dowsing was paid 6s 8d. It is believed that he broke up a beautiful alabaster reredos, a product of Norwich craftsmen. A few fragments were rescued and now stand in a niche in the chancel.

During the pastorate of Edward Powell (1843–1892) the church was extensively rebuilt using some of the original materials, notably the fine timber vault of the nave with its tie beams and angels. After Powell's death the tower collapsed and was rebuilt about 1894.

The village sign at Toft

The presence of a Methodist chapel in Toft bears witness to a well established history of Nonconformity in the village. Puritan ideas had taken deep root in the area at the time of the Civil War (1642–1645). In 1659 and other occasions John Bunyan preached in a barn in Toft. In 1860 a Primitive Methodist group was formed and in 1862 a foundation stone of a church was laid.

Toft is still a small village surrounded by farmland. In recent years part of this land has been converted into a fine golf course. With modern mechanisation only a handful of villagers bear any allegiance to the land. It is interesting to note that the Greenwich Meridian of zero longitude passes through the centre of the parish and a splendid sundial at the side of the road marks its position.

The village can boast one shop and one public house and many buildings of architectural interest. A very specialised small industrial development can be found tucked away off the High Street.

🍁 Trumpington

The shield with golden trumpets on the village sign is taken from the second oldest church brass in the country. This is the recumbent figure of crusader Sir Roger de Trumpington, 1289, in the parish church.

The village is now part of the city of Cambridge, but has many tangible links with its past. Traces of early settlements from the Iron Age and Roman periods on both sides of the river suggest that ancient trackways over the Gog Magog hills, from Essex and from the north west, converged at a point between Trumpington and Grantchester, with a ford over the river Cam. Byron's Pool is the site of the mill made famous by Chaucer in his *Canterbury Tales*.

Trumpington has been relatively populous since medieval times. The base of the mid 15th century cross was found when the foundations for the war memorial were dug in 1921 and it is now in the parish church under the tower. The village lock-up and pound were in the High Street and the pillory post from the lock-up is now in the Cambridge Folk Museum. The last time someone was locked up was in 1912, when a local policeman put in a man who was the worse for drink, to cool off. On unlocking the door the following day to take the man to court he was found to be in as bad a condition as the night before. It appears that his pals had kept him 'topped up' with beer administered through rubber tubing via the ventilator.

The tollgate keeper's house with weighbridge was sold in 1863 and converted into two cottages – now 'Weighbridge' and 'Tollbar' in the High Street. The remains of the weighbridge were found when the sewer was connected.

Whitelocks, a modern home for the elderly, stands in the High Street on the site of what was known as Whitelocks Yard. In 1724 George Whitelock willed his house to provide 34 poor households with coal, the coal to be of the cheapest! Coats and caps were also given annually to 18 poor people, the initials G.W. on them being a constant reminder to all of his generosity! Whitelock's house and malting were reconstructed in 1819 to be let as 20 cottages to poor people and the land to be let as allotments.

Anstey Hall and Trumpington Hall probably occupy the sites of earlier manor houses. The government acquired Anstey Hall Farm in 1950 as headquarters of the Plant Breeding Institute, but it has since been sold to public companies. Trumpington Hall has been in the Pemberton family since 1715. The Old House in Church Lane dates from the late 16th century and has crow-stepped gables at each end and small windows with labels or hood moulds.

Trumpington had its witch in the mid 1800s, one commonly known as Mother Sivill, who was periodically hauled before the magistrates to be punished for her ill-doings. It also had Henry Fawcett, the blind Postmaster General, who died in 1884 and is buried in the churchyard. The Fawcett School in the village is named after him.

Looking towards Cambridge from the Hauxton Road/Shelford Road junction, the High Street has changed a lot in the last 100 years; old pictures show cottages, green spaces, a few horse-drawn carts, one or two bicycles and cars. Today continuous traffic through the High Street has necessitated the installation of three sets of pedestrian traffic lights!

On the right side in 1947 a council estate and Fawcett School were built and on the site of the village green there are now shops and flats. On the opposite side of the road Bidwell's three-storey building, a large petrol station/garage and a chemist's shop occupy the site of a green corner where sheep once grazed. Opposite the war memorial a development of small neo-Georgian houses takes the place of a farmhouse and yard and a row of grey brick cottages. Adjacent to the war memorial is another Bidwell's office block, the site of the old blacksmith's yard.

The primary school is still in a rural position, however, and the

229

byroads towards the church and Grantchester retain a peaceful country atmosphere. Fortunately, too, extensive planting of mixed varieties of trees is overcoming the ravages of the 1970s Dutch elm disease.

❧ Tᴙᴅᴅ Sᴛ Gɪʟᴇs

As with many villages, Tydd St Giles is fairly quiet on the surface, but a great many inhabitants work hard behind the scenes to keep various activities going. Two of the main attractions are the Garden Fete, which is usually held in June, and the Flower Festival, which is now incorporated with the Harvest Festival in the autumn; proceeds from these events go to the Restoration Fund for repairs to the church.

The church is 12th century and built of Barnack stone and is one of three in the area with the tower standing apart from the main building. In the past money was raised, within the village, to repair the Great West Window, which was thought to have been designed by Alan de Walsingham who also designed the Lantern Tower in Ely Cathedral.

There are several fine old houses in the village, one of which is Tydd Manor, built in the 1600s and set among lots of beautiful trees. This used to be the venue for the Garden Fete. There are other houses in the village about the same age as the Manor. One is supposed to have been the home of a smuggler. Another house about a mile away is called Hannath Hall after a previous owner. This man was something of an eccentric and when his wife died he refused to have her buried, and had food and water placed beside her coffin for three weeks. Could it be her ghost which is supposed to haunt the Hall?

Tydd St Giles, which now has a much-used Community Centre, built in 1993, is set right in the north east corner of Cambridgeshire and is, and always has been, engaged mainly in agriculture. Allied to agriculture, in years past Tydd had its own wheelwright and this man's daughter carried on the trade after he died, virtually until her own demise. She is thought to have been the only lady wheelwright in the land. There was also a family of blacksmiths, two brothers, who were at the end of a 200 year line of smiths. The last one died in 1983. With his death the blacksmith's shop disappeared.

Going back further in time the name of John Lumpkin can be found. He was the last of his family. When his father died John was left one shilling and he gave this shilling to some travelling players on condition that they danced over his father's grave. He once made a wagon inside a shed and had to demolish the shed to get the wagon out. His end came when he fell from a wagon in a drunken state and was run over!

🍁 WARBOYS

Warboys is a typical fenland village, standing high on a ridge with extensive views towards Chatteris. It has many old buildings, notably the beautiful Manor House next to the 13th century parish church of St Mary Magdalene. The Manor was built in the early 17th century and has Dutch-style gables.

At the junction with High Street stands the Clock Tower commemorating the Jubilee of Queen Victoria in 1887. Travelling east along the High Street you will pass by the thatched White Hart public house, which has been renovated after a recent fire. There is a thriving bowls club and bar meals are available here. Next is the Methodist chapel, and a new development, Ashleigh Court, which offers sheltered accommodation for the over 55s.

Moving along you will find the Grace Baptist chapel and almost opposite there is the weir where people of all ages were baptised in large numbers in days past. Take the left fork of the road and you will find Station Road leading down the hill to the disused brickworks and the remains of the railway station. The brick pits are now used as a landfill site. On the right is Pingle Wood, pretty in the spring when it is filled with bluebells; it was once part of a much larger wood which ran along the ridge joining the Warboys Wood.

A second pub, the Royal Oak, stands at the Mill End side of the village. There is a good selection of small shops spread out along the High Street.

Warboys is famed for the execution of three witches in 1593. They were convicted of bewitching 14 people, but the charge was believed to have been trumped up.

A great deal of new building has taken place over the past 30 years and the population has risen rapidly. A community bus and a modern health centre are recent additions to the services available. With its own large primary school, library, sports field and Social Club plus several meeting halls, Warboys is a very busy place and has a large number of thriving organisations which are well supported.

🍁 WATERBEACH

Waterbeach is situated five miles north of Cambridge just off the A10 – originally a turnpike road with highwaymen, but now the main link for heavy transport between Ely, Kings Lynn and the ports on the Wash.

The village was originally called Bechea and is mentioned in Domesday Book with a population of 335; today this is in the order of 5,000 with a large proportion of the inhabitants commuting to Cambridge and London using the excellent train service. The village is centred around The Green, with its lime trees planted early in the 20th century, but housing estates have now been built on what were once green fields and grazing land. There is a small trading estate at the Denny End section of the village and several farms still exist on the fen lands to the north east.

The name Waterbeach is derived from the Old English 'beche' meaning brook. In 1238 it was known as Waterbeach. The names of Landbeach and Waterbeach became established when the fens

Waterbeach village sign

became wetter and the higher ground in Landbeach became even more desirable. Stock could still graze in Landbeach when Waterbeach was flooded. In 1770 historian Rev William Cole who had been curate at Waterbeach for three years moved to Milton. He wrote in his diary: 'Not being a water rat I have left Waterbeach and moved to higher ground in Milton.'

The remains of Car Dyke, an ancient canal built by the Romans, runs alongside the large recreation ground with its newly opened sports pavilion. The canal was originally built to serve as drainage, holding back the flood waters and probably for transporting grain to garrisons at Lincoln – recent excavations have revealed artefacts of the period and the remains of the original lock gate which linked it with the river Cam. The area has been marked by an inscribed stone erected by the Village Society in 1982.

Two abbeys exist with the parish boundaries – Waterbeach Abbey, which is now little more than undulations in the fields to the south of the parish church, and Denny Abbey, which was occupied at different times by the Benedictine monks, Knights Templars and the Franciscan Order of Minoresses (The Poor Clares). Denny Abbey, situated between Waterbeach and the hamlet of Chittering off the A10, is now controlled by English Heritage and scheduled as an ancient monument. It shares the site with the Farmland Museum, recently moved from Haddenham.

The oldest building in Waterbeach is the parish church of St John the Evangelist. There are some surviving Norman features which indicate that its origins were late 12th century although in general the architecture is Early English and Perpendicular. Much restoration and reconstruction has taken place over the centuries and is continuing. The bell and altar from the Fen Church, which was demolished after the floor collapsed during a harvest festival since in the 1960s, is in the south aisle.

Rev Charles Haddon Spurgeon, the famous Baptist preacher, was minister in Waterbeach during the 1850s when he was only 17. Later, he was invited back to lay the foundation stone of the present chapel which is named after him. It was built in 1863 when the dove house which the Baptist had been using was burnt down.

Another famous inhabitant of Waterbeach was John Denson who wrote *A Peasant's Voice* which gives a comprehensive picture of life in Waterbeach in the early 19th century. In 1823 he built his own cottage in Primrose Lane for £40. The cottage was demolished in 1952 but his great great grand-daughter still lives in Primrose Lane.

In 1970 the village school became a community primary school for the benefit of the area and in 1972 the Community Association was formed. This now consists of over 25 local organisations who are responsible for the 'Feast', which takes place on The Green at the beginning of June with stalls and a procession around the village. It is also responsible for the local prize winning magazine *Beach News* which is delivered to every household.

🍁 WATER NEWTON

This small village stands on the south bank of the river Nene between Alwalton and Stibbington. The A1 runs alongside the village, south to London and north to Stamford. The population is between 60 and 70.

Water Newton was a Roman settlement called Durobrivae (the fort at the ford). Ermine Street, forerunner of the A1, linked London with the fortresses at Lincoln and York. To guard the point where Ermine Street crossed the river Nene, a small five acre fort was erected, probably to house an auxiliary garrison.

Pottery kilns where calcite-gritted cooking pots were produced, have been found at Water Newton dating to the late 1st century AD. Clay and wood could be brought in by the Nene and the finished pots despatched by water.

A Christian silver hoard was found in February 1975, 27 silver objects and one gold. It is dated as not later than the 4th century AD. This discovery is the earliest group of Christian religious silver from the whole Roman Empire and is of international importance. Before the discovery of the Water Newton treasure, the two earliest known Christian treasures were found in Italy and Turkey, both of the 6th century. Water Newton silver may now be seen in the British Museum.

The parish church of St Remigius stands close to the south bank of the river Nene. St Remigius (AD 437–533) was a Roman and the Bishop of Rheims. His feast day is held on 1st October.

Three watermills at Water Newton are mentioned in the Domesday survey. The present mill, which replaced an older structure, bears the date 1791. It has been developed into five dwellings. Old barns and farm buildings have also been made into homes.

The manor house, now attached to the farm, and the house near the Old Rectory gates, both 17th century, were once coaching inns, the George and Chequers, with large stables. To the west of the village are old brickworks and about a quarter of a mile south an old gravel pit.

Water Newton did have a village stores which closed in 1963. Now there are no facilities in the village. The village school closed in 1945.

🍁 WERRINGTON

Werrington was an ancient settlement on the fringe of forest and fen. Of the several interpretations of the place-name, the most probable is 'the town of the Varini', a clan mentioned by Tacitus. Car Dyke, built by the Romans, still marks the eastern boundary of the parish. It is the only one of the surrounding hamlets to be included in the Domesday Book in 1086.

Until 1877 Werrington was in the parish of Paston. By an Order in Council of Queen Victoria dated 1853, the hamlets of Werrington and Walton were to form a separate parish on the death or retirement of the Rev J. Pratt of Paston, which occurred in 1877. The parish church of St John the Baptist was formerly a chapel of ease to Paston until this time. The church consists of a nave with aisles and a porch, and a chancel with vestries on the north side. The oldest parts of the building date from the early 12th century. Restorations in the late 19th and early 20th centuries have left the building as it is today.

In 1929 Werrington was included in the Soke of Peterborough city boundaries and a number of modern private housing areas were built during this period. Werrington has grown rapidly since that time, so that now there are three distinct neighbourhoods, each with its own shops, etc. These newer areas connect by footpaths, by cycle and by bus with the old village centre, now a conservation area and containing some attractive 17th century houses.

A new sports and community centre, alongside housing, was built on Foxcovert Road, to the north of Werrington village. This was one of the oldest roads in Peterborough and would have been the route Oliver Cromwell used to travel to Northborough Castle. On this road there were also many odd corners of woodlands, planted to give breeding cover for foxes, hence the name Foxcovert. In 1848 the Great Northern Railway loop line was constructed, cutting Foxcovert in two; the Werrington side of the wood was partly cleared and a Peterborough confectioner called Herbert (Toffee) Neaverson acquired it after a artesian bore had been sunk in 1899. He obtained pure natural soda water from the bore, and some Werrington residents still remember the little bottles of soda water sold from his bottling shed. Today only certain sections of the Foxcovert Road are open to vehicles; it is mainly used by walkers and cyclists who can enjoy the wild flowers and hedgerows in all seasons.

Werrington Feast, an ancient village tradition, took place on the first Sunday on or after 24th June, the Feast Day of St John the Baptist. This highlight of the village year is still celebrated as the Werrington Scout and Guide Carnival Saturday in June.

Werrington village through the ages has seen many changes. Through all these developments it has remained intact with a thriving social scene and a keen community spirit.

🍁 WEST WRATTING

The village of West Wratting was probably founded in about AD 800 and it is thought that the name 'Wratting' came from the Saxon word 'wraett' which means 'The place where the cross-wort (a type of bed-straw) grows'. It is quite a small village (population 300–400) in the south of the county, nestling against the Suffolk and Essex borders.

The Domesday Book mentions a church at West Wratting in 1086, probably built of wood. When the church of St Andrew was restored in 1730 it was found that an earlier church (believed to be Saxon) had stood on the same spot. Saxon foundations are within the walls of the nave, and a few pieces of Norman stonework are built into the present walls. The clergy and choir used to lead the congregation in a long crocodile through the village and allotments to bless the ground on Rogation Day. There is still a choir today, but the procession follows a restricted route.

The windmill is the oldest registered smock mill in England. This was probably built on the same spot as a former post mill and was last used for grinding corn in the 1920s.

The Hall is situated at the end of The Causeway next to the church. This is where Squire Frost lived and where he constructed a flying machine. This contraption was called an 'Ornithopta', and was built at the end of the 19th century, costing £1,000 and taking nine years to complete. Local women were employed to stitch goose feathers on the covering of the framework to make the wings and it was powered by a 5 hp steam engine. A charge of a farthing was made to view the machine, which proved too heavy to fly. Hardly leaving the ground, it crashed nearby in a field of cattle!

The Second World War brought many changes to West Wratting. An aerodrome was built on the common; Stirlings and Lancasters were among the bombers which flew on missions over Germany. There was also a searchlight battery nearby. Various army units were based either at the Hall (RAMC) or in tents in the meadow (RASC). Soldiers were always complaining about the plague of earwigs which tormented them at night. Members of the Eighth Army came to West Wratting on their return from North Africa. The Park House was used to billet toddlers evacuated from London. Most householders in the village took in evacuees. The three pubs in the village quickly sold out of beer with all the extra customers available! There were rumours that spies were operating from the Lamb – they supposedly had a radio transmitter, but one night they disappeared and nothing more was heard of them. Only one stick of bombs was dropped in the village throughout the war, missing all buildings and landing in the fields.

A folk myth inherited from Viking settlers may account for the tradition that the countryside between West Wratting and Balsham is haunted by the 'Shug Monkey'. The creature, either ghost or demon, is said to be jet black and shaggy haired with a monkey face and staring eyes. There is also a tale of 'The White Lady' who supposedly walks from Concordia House (on the common) to the woods surrounding the park.

🍁 WICKEN

Wicken is an attractive small village of about 700 people, including its hamlets of Padney and Upware. It has four village greens, a pretty pond, a pump, a war memorial and the remains of a market cross. At one end of the village is the 13th century church and at the other end is the Methodist chapel. In between are a butcher's shop, a car repair workshop, a hairdresser, a blacksmith, a pottery and a thatched pub. In fact, several of the houses are thatched and those round the pond date back to the early 1600s.

There are two groups of almshouses. The benefactress, Mary Hatch, also started the old dame school (now closed) and various charities, such as an annual contribution of 10 shillings' worth of coal, half a crown for blankets and a yard of calico for the poor.

The Victorian Mission Hall is in the middle of the village and the centre of village life. It has been modernised and extended with money raised by the whole village and has recently been awarded a grant for new kitchen and servery facilities.

Not far from the Mission Hall is the 19th century mill, which is being restored with a grant from English Heritage and is open to the public on some summer weekends.

The church houses the tomb of Henry Cromwell, Lord Protector of Ireland and son of Oliver Cromwell. Henry and his wife Elizabeth (also buried in the church) lived a mile outside the village at Spinney Abbey, where the ghostly singing of the monks who inhabited the abbey long ago can be heard on Easter Day. The monks used to walk to church along the main road, now the A1123.

Behind the church is Wicken Hall, a beautiful mellow building. The largest house in Wicken, it still retains traces of its original moat.

A major tourist attraction is Wicken Fen, haunt of birds, reeds, wild flowers and insects – especially insects! Indeed, it claims to have the largest mosquitoes in the country. The Fen is run by the National Trust who do guided tours in the summer months. It has the longest boardwalk in the county, so disabled visitors and mothers with pushchairs can enjoy the peace and timeless beauty.

🍁 WILBURTON

Evidence of early habitation has been found in the village and surrounding fens: flint axeheads, a hoard of bronze spears and swords, a gold torque and Roman coins.

The village is on the high ride of the Isle of Ely, much higher than the fenland. It is still an agricultural and fruit growing area but only a few people now work on the land. Most people find employment in Cambridge or Ely. There has been a decline in fruit growing and many acres of fruit trees have been pulled up and returned to arable crops.

The church is situated at the west end of the High Street. This dates from the 13th century. Opposite the church is the Rectory which was the home of the late Lord of the Manor, Mr B.S. Pell.

Bishop Alcock of Ely was Lord of the Manor from 1486 to 1500. He entertained King Henry VII and the young Prince Henry when they came to visit the shrine of St Etheldreda at Ely. The Berristead, formerly the Manor House, is in Station Road and opposite the recreation ground. A new Manor House was built nearby in parkland; it is now a special school with day children and boarders from all over the country. Other houses of interest are Bell Gables, a later 17th century farmhouse of brick with curved gables near the church. Not far away is The Grange, a timber-framed house, and The Tythe House in School Lane is another timbered house with a thatched roof. The Old School was built in 1855 and stands in a prominent position at the junction of School Lane and the High Street. It comprises a private house and the schoolroom, which is now an office.

A new primary school was built in 1958 at the far end of Carpond Lane, and currently has about 100 children attending. The older children in the main go to the Witchford Village College.

The Baptist chapel is midway along the High Street. It has a large schoolroom at the rear for extra meetings. Next to the chapel is the village hall, let for all village activities and under the control of the Parish Council. At the rear of the hall is a Social Club.

Before the war there were many shops and businesses – three public houses, garage, blacksmith, baker, hairdresser, butcher, grocer, post office and carpenter – but now there is only the post office, one public house and two garages.

Many new houses have been built recently, including two old people's groups of flats – Lucas Court and Bakery Close which is warden controlled.

🍁 WILLINGHAM

Perched on the southern edge of the fens at all of 22 feet above sea level, Willingham is protected from flooding by the high banks of the river Great Ouse and the artificial New and Old Bedford cuts beyond. Older Willingham people will tell you of the inundation of 1947, when the Ouse bank – partly of medieval construction– gave way at Over and flooded large parts of both parishes. At Easter 1998 young and old were able to look on in wonder at the containment of extraordinarily high water levels which wrought much destruction upstream at Bedford and Northampton. The rivers hold important nature reserves and are used throughout the year for fishing and by pleasure craft.

Willingham originated as a small farming community of a few families in the 6th century, led by a man called Wifel (now evolved to Will) after whom they named themselves. Archaeologists have lately revealed extensive traces of their homes close to the centre of the village. Simple houses, rectangular in plan and built of rows of earth-set posts supporting both walls and roofs, provided shelter for these Angles and Saxons and their stock. They also grew crops and harvested the riches of the undrained fen where they probably had a sanctuary for pagan gods.

In a later, still Anglo-Saxon, century, a church was founded right on the fen edge by the side of a creek which later dried out to become a village street. Willingham church, like others on the southern fen edge, kept a watchful eye on the unmentionable horrors of the watery wastes, a prey to the imagination even down to our time.

Besides the fine medieval church with splendid hammerbeam roof and fine wall paintings, the village has Baptist Tabernacle, Methodist and Salvation Army congregations in their own excellent purpose-built places of worship. All regularly come together to share services and produce a joint magazine.

Readily drawn to nearby centres (Cambridge, St Ives etc) for work, recreation and shopping, Willingham people are yet sufficiently numerous (3,500 and rising), independent and resolute to sustain many a local shop and business and to withstand pressure always to conform to the will of outsiders ('foreigners'). Local authorities just do not seem to understand this.

Although most Willingham people now work outside the parish, several farmers continue to work the land around the village. With scarcely a cow or sheep, pig or chicken to their name, their income comes overwhelmingly from arable agriculture. Yet there are a growing number of horse keepers in the parish, in part satellites to the world of Newmarket racing. Some villagers still work in horticulture – orchards and plants for cut flowers – although this is now but a shadow of a once substantial local industry.

There has been uninterrupted continuity of education in

Willingham since 1593. The oldest school in the area was the Subscription School, founded by the villagers rather than one person. A public subscription was taken in the village with contributions ranging from three farthings to twenty pounds. The money was invested in land to provide income for a master and one or two pupil teachers at all times.

In 1856 the British School was opened. In 1902 all Church schools were taken over by the School Board. Nonconformists in the village (of whom there had always been a great number) decided that they did not want the Board School and preferred their own. They 'passively resisted' paying the part of the rate set for education. Nor would they pay fines. In the end some of their possessions were distrained and put up for auction. It happened that the auctioneer sympathised with the 'resisters'. So not only did he give his services free but he also 'knocked down' the goods for surprisingly little money. And most of the 'resisters' bought each others' goods! Today, a recently refurbished and enlarged new primary school stands in a large open space with playground and playing field.

🍁 WIMBLINGTON

Situated between March and Doddington, Wimblington has a population of 1,500 and each year is expanding with new houses and council bungalows. This is a quiet village but certainly not a sleepy one.

In its early days, Wimblington consisted of a few small dwellings belonging to the lord of the manor of Doddington and before getting their own work done villagers had to do so much for him. Their work was concerned with animal husbandry, fishing, wild-fowling, eel catching and repairing buildings. The main diet consisted of wild duck and fish, varied with seasonal lamb and mutton. Venison was a rarity imported from Huntingdonshire and Northamptonshire.

A great deal of building went on in Georgian times and some of the larger houses are still in use. The oldest house is actually 17th century (North House) and then there is a Georgian pedimented house (Addison House), a manor house and Hill House.

In 1809 a chapel was built in Chapel Lane and in 1850 another (Primitive Methodist) in Hook. These two served for several years but eventually a new one, built in 1877, became the only Methodist church. The parish church was consecrated in 1874 and by the end of the 1800s both churches had Sunday schools and choirs.

At this time the village had many tradesmen and was self sufficient – cobbler, carpenters, butcher, baker, grocer, greengrocer, milkman, blacksmith and dressmaker. There was a post office and cycle repair shop, an undertaker and Mr E. Bradshaw, a carpenter, who made the coffins for people buried by the parish. There was always a lady to attend births and deaths, the best remembered being Granny Bradshaw and Mrs Cornish. Now most of these have gone, and the railway, but there is still a post office, two general stores, a butcher and a newsagent.

This village is fortunate in having a very good school, in existence since 1802. It was an endowed school from the will of Mr Thomas Eaton, who wanted the village children to learn at least reading, writing and arithmetic. It was to be a mixed school of 40 boys and girls, girls leaving at 13 and boys at 14 years. Today it is a popular school where the children learn much more, but the fund from the original endowment buys many things they would otherwise not have.

The story of Wimblington would not be complete without a mention of 'The Park Carnations. This was a hackney pony bred by his own stable from his prize winning stud by Mr W. Bellamy of Park House. This pony won every event it attended in the country and even swept the board at Olympia. It was so good to work and to look at that Bertram Mills wanted to buy it for his circus.

🍁 WIMPOLE

Wimpole is derived from 'Wina's pool'. Wina was a bondsman living near a pond or a pool which was located near the village's only claim to fame – Wimpole Hall, now owned by the National Trust and giving new life to the village. Wimpole is only a small parish in size, 2,468 acres with a population of approximately 200–300.

The original village of Old Wimpole and New Wimpole, built in 1845 by the 4th Earl of Hardwicke to house workers of the estate, are both closely connected with the Hall which in the past provided most of the employment. Now the National Trust provides a few jobs but most people commute to other villages, for example to cement works at Barrington and asbestos works at Whaddon.

A generation ago it was a thriving village with two public houses, a smithy and a church school attended by 80 children. The Hall, brickyard and woodyard gave employment. Wimpole and Arrington, which also joins the estate, had a cricket team. A shoe mender, John Reed, who was deaf and dumb walked four miles from Arrington every day to his shop in Wimpole, especially built for him by Lord Clifden.

Now the village has only one garage, which must be a sign of the times, and a small woodyard. The school was closed some years ago in the 1960s, the children going to a new school in Orwell.

The church of St Andrew is two miles from the village, near the site of the original village next to the mansion house.

The Hall as it is today was built in 1632 by Sir Thomas Chicheley. Lord Radnor planted two miles of elms but these fell victim to Dutch elm disease. They have now been replanted by the National Trust. A later owner was Lord Harley, 2nd Earl of Oxford, after whom Harley Street and Oxford Street in London were named. The grounds were landscaped by Capability Brown, and in 1843 Queen Victoria and Prince Albert stayed there. Later owners were Lord Hardwicke and Viscount Clifden, whose son sold it to the last owners Captain and

Mrs. Bambridge – daughter of Rudyard Kipling.

From 1939 to 1945 the house was requisitioned and the army moved into the house and park. Now the National Trust house and farm attract thousands of visitors each year.

❧ WISTOW

Wistow is a pretty village set in a valley with a brook running by, just off the Warboys to Ramsey road. It was an important village in Domesday times. Then it had a mill, church and brook.

The church is still part of the village but the rector is now shared by Warboys, Broughton, Bury and Wistow.

The village has a shop cum post office, one public house, the Three Horseshoes, and a village hall. Children from the village are bussed to Upwood and Ramsey for school, but Wistow does have a thriving play group. There are regular buses to local towns as well as a weekly community bus.

The Parish Council plays an active role in the village and provides an attractive play area. Farming is still the main industry of the village.

❧ WITCHFORD

Witchford is a village on the A142 three miles west of Ely, with a population of 1,850. In AD 607 St Augustine built a small church 'where the Wyche elm grows by the ford' and called it St Andrew's after his church in Rome. The present St Andrew's church dates from 1376.

In 1875 a foundation stone laying ceremony was performed for the building of the Baptist church, when a copy of the Church Articles was placed under the stone.

In 1844 the Rev Rackham gave the land on which to build a

village school. Money was raised for this purpose and part of this school, together with modern extensions, makes up the present-day primary school for about 290 children.

The village college stands on the site of a Second World War RAF camp. Building started in 1959 and it has been extensively extended to cater for 815 students from 11 years to 16 years. This college is also used for adult education classes, sports etc.

St Andrew's Hall, which was built in 1900 from money raised by the village community, stands on the site of the old village pound.

Facilities include a post office stores, village shop and two garages. Light industry in the village has recently been increased by the provision of a small Business Park.

❦ WITTERING

The village has been overtaken by the 20th century RAF base, known locally as the 'Home of the Harriers', and now only a few old cottages are left beside the outstanding Saxon church, whose proportions are tall and narrow. There is distinctive Saxon long and short work and the massive chancel arch is most impressive. An aisle was added on the north side in later years and the tower and spire in the 14th century.

❦ WOODHURST

The village is situated north of Huntingdon and St Ives, reached by a byroad between the A141 and B1040. It is 100 ft above sea level and is one of the best examples of a ring village surviving in England, practically unaltered in shape since it was first founded in thick woodland some 2,000 or more years ago. It was established along a trackway through forest, by widening the road at a convenient place on both sides, forming an oblong space in which the village was built.

The road was then divided when it entered the village to run round the perimeter until it came to the exit, thus forming a ring around the houses and small fields it enclosed. At the entry and exit would be gates or some protection and along the outer edge of the encircling road would be a stockade to keep wild animals and would-be intruders out.

The church and manor house came centuries later and had to be built outside the ring as there was no room for them inside the ring fence. Other houses followed later. The ring road and the original shape is thus preserved.

During building in 1949 a number of skeletons and fragments of pottery of Saxon origin were found.

The oldest part of the church dates back to the 11th century and the building has many interesting features. The spire has a pepperpot shape and it is thought there is only one other like it in the country. The village population at one time rose to 500 with seven public houses to serve them, but following two years of bad harvests it dwindled to 200 and remains near that figure.

In November 1834 a fire started in one of the farms and devastated almost half the village, leaving 12 families, all with children, homeless. It is reported that some of the village labourers appeared indifferent to the results of the blaze in as much as some were intoxicated and some engaged in pugilistic contests!

The custom of celebrating the festival of the church's patron saint – St John the Baptist – was revived in 1949 and is today expanded into a Feast Week sponsored by an energetic Village Hall Management Committee with a view to raising funds towards the upkeep of the village hall, having already achieved the building of the hall itself. They also arrange many other events in the village.

There is a charity in the village called Clay Pits Charity. Some fields are hired out to farmers and the money received is given to elderly folk in the village towards their coal or electricity bills each year. This was left by an elderly gentleman some years ago and is still continued.

🍁 WOODWALTON

Woodwalton is a small village to the north of Huntingdon mentioned in the Domesday Book of 1086 under the name of 'Waltune' but archaeological finds suggest a much earlier settlement. An area of some 5,000 acres, it is divided equally between black fenland in the north and gault clay in the south, rising to 130 feet above sea level and mostly used for arable farming.

Only one really old building survives, St Andrew's church, which is now redundant but burials still take place very occasionally in the churchyard. Built in the mid 13th century, it was closed in 1967 and has since suffered extensive vandalism. The two 13th century lancet stained glass windows can now be seen in the Ely Cathedral Glass Museum. The large Victorian rectory is a private residence.

The village consists of two areas, Church End to the north and the main village to the south, with what was the school and schoolhouse, founded in 1860 and closed 1963, and the church midway between. When the railway was constructed in 1850 the village was further divided in an easterly/westerly direction. Like most villages there are few of the original families living here.

Unfortunately the village shop closed some years ago but there is still a village hall which was built, partly by public subscription, in 1949, this being quite an achievement for such a small population. Only one public house survives, the Elephant and Castle, the other, the Rose and Crown, having been converted to a private dwelling many years ago.

Of interest is the large stand of horse chestnut trees which is thought to have been planted in the late 19th century and still provides a healthy crop of conkers to the delight of the children. On the original village green stands the war memorial in memory of those killed in two World Wars, together with the base of an ancient cross. Neither the date nor the origin of this is known.

Nearby is Monks Wood, a large wooded area noted for butterflies which is overseen by the Institute of Terrestrial Ecology. Woodwalton Fen, to the north of the village, is reached via Ramsey Heights and is now a nature reserve but at one time was a source of fuel for heating the local houses in the form of turf. This is a remnant of the fen which covered huge areas and is now enclosed by clay banking to keep it as a wetland in which fen fauna and flora can flourish. It is open to the public.

🍁 YAXLEY

The village of Yaxley is reputed to be the largest village in England, which these days could be a disputed fact, for due to the large number of new housing estates plus factories that have been built in Yaxley, it now seems to be more a small township. However, many of the old buildings in Main Street have been skilfully preserved and one is still able to find the peace and characteristic beauty of the old village.

Built on the edge of the fens, Yaxley has some of the most fertile land in the country. However, at the opposite side of the village there are many seams of clay, which have been quarried and used in the making of bricks – hence the features of the boundary skylines are tall chimneys, which now are belching less smoke as the industry declines.

The history of wars is also written into Yaxley for the fens were used as a waterway to convey prisoners during the early 19th century Anglo-French wars. Flat-bottomed boats were landed at a point along Main Street and the prisoners marched up Church Street to their camp at Norman Cross. It appears that they found kindness in at least one person during their internment for a plaque is to be found in the church commemorating the life of an officer. The cost of this memorial had been borne by many prisoners out of their meagre pocket-money. During the Second World War history was repeated when a prisoner of war camp was built in the village. This was mainly for Italian prisoners who were either put to work on the land or in the brick kilns. There was no plaque of commemoration for this period but many Italians stayed in the community after VE Day.

The largest part of Main Street contains listed buildings and on the small village green (where once the inhabitants held a market) one can still see the old village water pump and also an Edward VII pillar box, which is still in use.

At the present day there are three schools in the village for children up to the age of 11. In the Main Street of Yaxley there is a well equipped Fire Station which employs both permanent and retained firemen – it has grown to such an extent that it has its own social club on the premises. Besides an excellent Health Centre, Yaxley can boast a Senior Citizens' Retirement Centre (where a day centre for the elderly is also organised) and an adult handicapped home from where supervision is also given to five houses around the village where handicapped men and women make their home life.

The fens were drained in Cromwellian times by Vermuyden, and now there are beautiful views of acres of fertile crops stretching many miles to adjoining villages. These viewpoints are found on the hillsides leading up from the old village and also from bedroom and attic windows along Main Street. On a clear day it is a glorious sight!

🍁 YELLING

At the beginning of the 20th century there were about 58 families living in the village of Yelling. It was a thriving community with six farmers, a butcher, a cobbler, a pub, a school, a blacksmith, its own vicar, a post office, a shop and a wheelwright and undertaker. The majority of cottages standing then housed several families in a terrace, but today they have been modernised and altered to provide much more spacious homes. Most residents of the village then worked on the land.

Some new houses were built between the wars to replace some cottages which had fallen down. In 1930 the vicar died and the

251

parish was taken over by the vicar of Graveley. Some of the craftsmen died or moved away in this period and were not replaced. No electricity was in the village then and fresh water arrived once a day in a lorry. You put out buckets for water at your gate; some days you got one bucketful, sometimes two!

After the Second World War another 14 houses were built, and electricity, piped water and the telephone were on their way. In the 1950s there was still a pub, post office, shop, butcher and school – though by then the school covered only the primary years and the older children were taken by bus the eight miles to Gamlingay.

By 1970 the only remaining amenity was the butcher's shop. The village school had finally closed but the building was bought for the village, to be a village hall and social centre.

It is now rare to find employment in the village and residents commute in all directions. Farm boundaries have changed considerably, and of the six farmhouses only two now house a farming family.

INDEX